HOW TO CHEAT IN BLENDER 2.7x

HOW TO CHEAT IN BLENDER 2.7x

Alan Thorn

CRC Press
Taylor & Francis Group
Boca Raton London New York

CRC Press is an imprint of the
Taylor & Francis Group, an **informa** business

A CHAPMAN & HALL BOOK

CRC Press
Taylor & Francis Group
6000 Broken Sound Parkway NW, Suite 300
Boca Raton, FL 33487-2742

© 2017 by Taylor & Francis Group, LLC
CRC Press is an imprint of Taylor & Francis Group, an Informa business

International Standard Book Number-13: 978-1-4987-6451-3 (paperback)

Library of Congress Cataloging-in-Publication Data

Names: Thorn, Alan.
Title: How to cheat in Blender 2.7x / Alan Thorn.
Description: Boca Raton : Taylor & Francis, CRC Press, [2017]
Identifiers: LCCN 2016035598 | ISBN 9781498764513 (pbk. : alk. paper)
Subjects: LCSH: Blender (Computer file) | Computer animation. | Computer games--Programming.
Classification: LCC TR897.72.B55 T45 2017 | DDC 777/.7--dc23
LC record available at https://lccn.loc.gov/2016035598

Visit the Taylor & Francis Web site at
http://www.taylorandfrancis.com

and the CRC Press Web site at
http://www.crcpress.com

Contents

Author

Alan Thorn is a game developer, author, and educator with 15 years of industry experience. He makes games for PC desktops, mobiles, and virtual reality. He founded Wax Lyrical Games and created the award-winning game *Baron Wittard: Nemesis of Ragnarok*, working as designer, programmer, and artist. He has written 15 technical books on game development and presented 10 video training courses, covering gameplay programming, Unity development, and 3D modeling. He is also a visiting lecturer at the National Film and Television School for the Game Design and Development master's degree program.

1

Interface Cheats

Sometimes, power consists not so much in *what* you do but in the way you do it. This is especially true when it comes to using the Blender interface. Blender offers lots of options and features for getting work done (like the modeling, sculpting, and animation tools), but these together are only a part of the whole story. To use these features optimally and most effectively, you'll want to customize the Blender interface to complement the tools you need and the purpose they should serve. This chapter focuses on the many ways you can change or use the Blender interface (both minor and major) to enhance your workflow. Some of these cheats will be "Did you know" tips, whereas others will explore potentially game-changing techniques.

Interface Cheats

1.1 Factory Reset ▶1.1

Perhaps you need to demo your work to others from within the Blender interface, without that crazy user interface scheme you've been using. Or maybe you've changed so many application preferences and can't remember what you've changed, and you just want to reset Blender back to its defaults to start afresh. You can do that with a Factory Reset. Simply select *File > Load Factory Settings*,

1.1

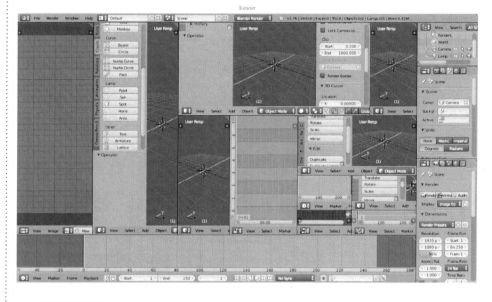

1.2

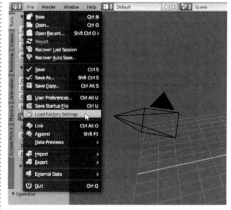

as shown in **1.2**. So simple an option yet so commonly undiscovered! ▶1.2

WARNING. Loading the factory default settings will reset all user interface customization, preferences, and control scheme settings back to their original values. Once reset, Blender will work as it did when first installed. Of course, a Factory Reset will *not* remove or invalidate any saved Blender scene files.

1.2 Last-Session Recovery ▶1.3

Occasionally you'll exit Blender without saving your hard work and changes. This may have been done intentionally or by accident. But, in any case, you may later wish that, after all, you'd actually kept all those changes. If this ever happens, then all is not necessarily lost! You can always try *recovering the last session*.

Every time you exit Blender, the active scene is automatically saved to an internal scene file representing the last active session. When you select the option *File > Recover Last Session* from the application menu, Blender loads that last session back as though it were any other saved file. This can be a fast and effective way to recover the last scene you were working on. ▶1.4

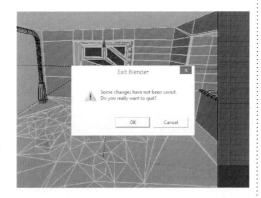

1.3

1.4

1 Interface Cheats

1.3 Recovering Overwritten Files ▶1.5

Saving your work regularly is good practice, but there are still dangers involved with saving, especially when using the *File > Save* command. After all, you can easily *save over* previous work, overwriting the original file. Now there isn't necessarily anything wrong in doing that—in fact, such frugal saving can optimize hard drive space, leaving you with fewer files. But this strategy only makes sense when you know that the original work will never be needed again. Unfortunately, you can't always be so certain. That's why you'll sometimes want to revert back to earlier versions of your project, retrieving models or data that once existed.

1.5

Thankfully, Blender backs up previous versions of your project every time you save. The backups are auto-generated alongside your main file (in the same folder) and take the extension of .blend1, .blend2, and so on. Perhaps you've seen these files before. Their total number depends on how many backups Blender is configured to make. The file with the extension .blend1 represents your project *one* save ago, the extension .blend2 represents it *two* saves ago, and so on. ▶1.6

1.6

To configure the number of backups, if you want any, select *File > User Preferences* from the application menu (to access the *User Preferences* window), and then choose the *File* tab. From the *File* tab, set the number of backups in the *Save Versions* field. ▶1.7

1.7

After the *Save Versions* field has been set and the user preferences are saved, Blender automatically creates backup files on each *Save* operation. Just click *File > Save* from the application menu. ▶1.8

1.8

T--I--P

An alternative *Save* method, in addition to automatic Blender backups, is *incremental saving*. This method requires you to use the *Save As* command cleverly: manually appending numbers to the ends of file names, indicating the order in which your file was saved (e.g., Myscene_01, Myscene_02, and Myscene_03). This lets you identify the latest version of a Blender project just by the file name (the latest version is the file with the highest number). Conveniently, Blender can also apply incremental saving semi-automatically. To achieve this, click *File > Save As* from the application menu, and from the *Save* dialog, just click the + button to automatically append an incremented number to the end of the file name. Blender does the counting for you!

1.4 Start-Up Files ▶1.9

Every time you start Blender, the start-up scene is opened. By default, this scene is minimal, featuring a camera, a lamp, and a cube, presented in the default interface layout. In many cases, this represents an acceptable starting point for your own work. But sometimes, you'll want more, or just something different. Specifically, when working on larger, team projects that span multiple scenes and files, it's helpful to establish a consistent start-up file for everybody so that everybody begins from the same place and with the same settings. You can achieve this by creating a completely new start-up file with your own configuration and data, and Blender will load this file every time you start

1.9

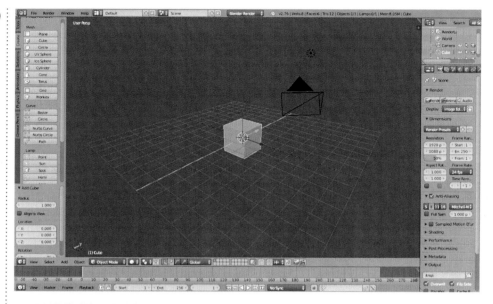

1.10

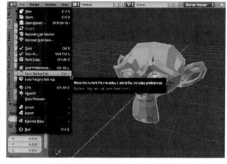

the program. To achieve this, open the file you want to use as a new start-up file, and then from the application menu, select *File > Save Startup File* (or press *Ctrl + U*). ▶1.10

1.11

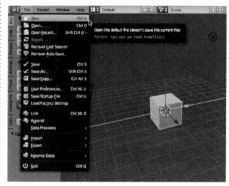

1.5 Multiple Scenes ▶1.11

It's easy to think of Blender, and Blender files, as being *scene based*. That is, one Blender file = one scene. Understanding Blender like this typically leads you to choose *File > New* from the application menu every time you want to make a new scene. But this is not really the way Blender works. Blender is a *project-based* application, and each Blender file may therefore contain *multiple* scenes. This is useful to know because you'll often work on projects, like games or movies, that feature many *related* scenes—scenes that are practically separate and yet belong together conceptually in an important sense. In these cases, it makes sense to create *one* project with *multiple* scenes.

You can add a new scene to the active project by simply clicking the *New Scene (+)* button from the application tool bar, close to the interface preset options. ▶1.12

1.12

After an additional scene has been added to the project, you can easily switch between scenes from the Hierarchy Panel. Just click the scene, and Blender switches automatically—although for larger and more complex scenes, a switch may take some loading time. When changing between scenes, all objects and settings for Blender will change too, depending on the contents of the scene. ▶1.13

1.13

If you can't see your scenes listed in the Hierarchy Panel, you can change the *Search Filter* to control the kinds of objects that are displayed. To view all scenes, change the filter to *All Scenes*. ▶1.14

1.14

1.6 Asset Sharing and Reusing

Reusing assets, meshes, and scenes is a common need for artists and teams. It's an essential part of working cleverly with Blender. When you spend hours, days, and perhaps even weeks of valuable time making a fantastic-looking asset, you'll want to reuse it elsewhere. The alternative is to model the same thing from scratch again every time you need it, which is terribly wasteful. In addition, you'll need to share assets with other team members, letting them reuse your work, saving them a ton of time. Blender comes with many features that help you achieve this. Let's see these in turn.

1.6.1 Import and Export

Need to migrate your assets out of Blender and into the hands of other people using different applications, like other modeling software or game engines? Then you'll need to *Export* your work. Alternatively, if other artists need you to modify or use what they've made in external software, then you'll need to *Import* their work into Blender. The import/export process relies on data interchange file formats, which allow data to be transferred between programs, many of which support different features and understand data differently. There are many formats available, and you'll need to negotiate with others about the right format for your needs. Blender can import and export data via the application's file menu. Simply choose *File > Import* to import data from an external file, or *File > Export* to save content from Blender to an external file. One of the most common uses of exporting is to save content to a game engine, like Unity or Unreal (the FBX export option is the most common format for this purpose). ▶1.15

1.15

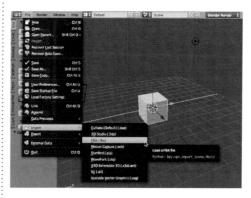

1.6.2 Appending

Maybe you just want to transfer assets between Blender files. For example, maybe you want to take a copy of a model or asset from one Blender file and transfer it to a different file, one that can be edited, moved, and changed just like any regular object. To achieve this, you can use the *Append* option. This can be accessed via the file menu, using the command *File > Append*. ▶1.16

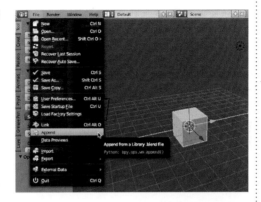

1.16

When you choose *File > Append*, the Open Dialog appears, allowing you to choose a Blender file from which data should be imported. However, once a Blender file is chosen, the Open Dialog allows you to dig even deeper into the contents of the Blender file itself. A Blender file has a hierarchical structure, much like the folder-file structure on a hard drive. To import mesh data, you'll typically choose the Object folder, to pick the object to be imported. ▶1.17

1.17

After an object is appended to the scene, it exists within the scene as a separate and independent object that can be edited and transformed, much like any other object in the scene. ▶1.18

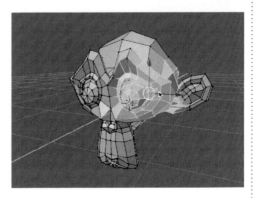

1.18

Interface Cheats

1.6.3 Linking

With the *Append* command, an asset from one file can be copied and added to another file as an independent asset. Once added, the appended object can be edited and transformed like any other object. It takes on a life of its own. The *Link* command, conversely, allows an object from an external file to be appended to the active file (just like the *Append* command), but the imported object cannot be edited, and it retains its connection to the original file. This is useful because any changes made to the asset in the original file will be updated and reflected automatically in all other files wherever there is a *link*.

This allows you to work with assets from other artists, and those same artists may continue to modify the asset in their own files, and these modifications will always be propagated back to all the links. To link an asset from a file (adding it to the active scene), choose *File > Link* from the application menu. ▶1.19

After selecting *File > Link* from the application menu, the Open Dialog is displayed, allowing you to select a Blender file for importing. As with the *Append* command, you can dig down deeper into the Blender file itself, viewing its hierarchical structure for objects to link. To link to a mesh, open the Objects folder, and pick the mesh to link into the active file. ▶1.20

Linked objects are highlighted in blue, indicating their dependent nature. By default, linked objects cannot be transformed or edited. That is, you cannot move, rotate, or scale them; and you cannot edit their inner structure, such as vertices, edges, and faces. All these properties are controlled from the source file from which the object is linked. If you want to transform the object (move, rotate, or scale) while still keeping the mesh data linked to the source, you should select the linked object and then choose *Object > Make Local > Selected Objects* from the viewport menu. When you do this, the imported object is still linked to the original, but the position orientation and scale properties become independent and local to the file. ▶1.21

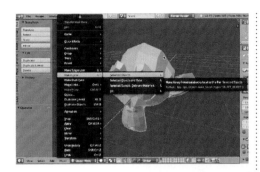

1.21

1.7 User Preferences

The Blender *User Preferences* window offers a comprehensive array of settings, which control how the application works, including user interface themes, input and controls, and hardware settings. Most of the settings are well documented. Their names clearly indicate their purpose. But some are lesser known and more obscure, and yet they offer impressive performance enhancements. The following subsections consider some of these settings. To access the *User Preferences* window, either click *File > User Preferences* from the application menu, or else convert any panel into a *User Preferences* window by clicking the *Panel Mode* icon and selecting the *User Preferences* option from the drop-down list. ▶1.22

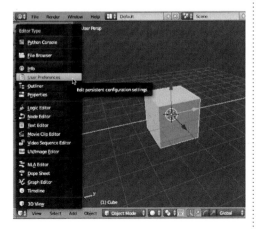

1.22

1.7.1 The Compute Device and Rendering Performance

By default, Blender is configured to run on as many different hardware configurations as possible, from old to new hardware. This means the default settings largely have hardware support in mind, as opposed to optimal performance on specific, high-powered hardware. For this reason, if you have a high-powered gaming or graphics card, you can often improve Blender's performance by adjusting the default settings. Specifically, the *System* tab in the *User Preferences* window influences Blender run-time performance. Perhaps the most important setting among these is the *Compute Device*, found at the bottom-left side of the *System* tab. This controls whether Blender renders and calculates scene data on the CPU (slower) or using the available graphics hardware (faster). When the *Compute Device* is set to *None*, the CPU is used by default. Older

1.23

hardware may only offer this option. However, the *Compute Device* can be set to *CUDA* on Windows and to *OpenCL* on Mac and Linux. When choosing either of the latter options, you can select your graphics hardware from the drop-down list below. It's a good idea to always choose either *CUDA* or *OpenCL*, as this significantly improves Blender's performance. ▶1.23

1.24

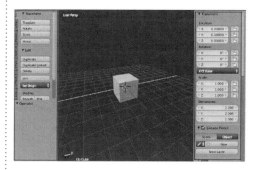

1.7.2 Region Overlap

Here's an interesting tip. Normally, when displaying the N Panel or the Tool Box, the contents of the 3D viewport shift automatically to accommodate interface resizing, as additional panels slide into view and compete for screen space. This is the default behavior. ▶1.24

However, shifts and changes in the viewport can be distracting, especially during texture painting and sculpting work. You can easily change this behavior, however, by enabling the *Region Overlap* option, available from the *System* tab in the *User Preferences* window. When enabled, on-screen panels (like the N Panel and the Tool Box) will instead overlap the views they slide into. You'll notice a semitransparent look to the panels too. ▶1.25

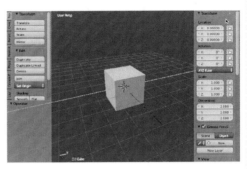

1.25

1.7.3 Auto-Perspective

There are many viewing angles for the 3D view panel: *Front*, *Side*, *Top*, *Down*, and *User*. Each of these angles can be in one of two main modes too: *Perspective* and *Orthographic*. You can easily switch between viewing angles using keyboard hot keys or menu options. You can also change between viewing modes, using the option *View > View Persp/Ortho* from the 3D menu. ▶1.26

1.26

In Blender, the typical workflow is to use hot keys for switching between viewing angles when working on a scene. Normally, you'll want to view *User Perspective* views and *Custom Camera* views in *Perspective* mode and other views (front, sides, up, and down) in *Orthographic* mode, free from perspective distortions. To have this set automatically, you should enable the option *Auto Perspective* from the *Interface* tab in the *User*

1.27

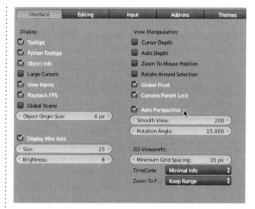

Preferences window. When this is enabled, Blender automatically switches the *User Perspective* and *Camera* views into *Perspective* mode and every other view into *Orthographic* mode. ▶**1.27**

1.28

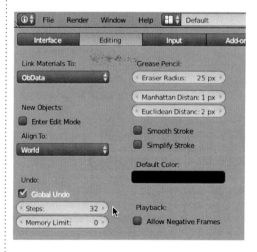

1.7.4 Undo Limit

While you are working—whether you're modeling, texturing, sculpting, or something else—Blender may keep track of up to 30 versions of your Blender project for maintaining an Undo hierarchy so you can perform multiple Undo steps if needed. Having multiple Undo steps can be very useful, but it also consumes memory. For this reason, try reducing the total number of Undo steps permitted to the minimum necessary for your work. To do this, set the number of *Undo Steps* from the *Editing* tab of the *User Preferences* window. By default, the value is 32, though I often go as low as 10. ▶**1.28**

1.8 Multimonitor Setup

The Blender interface *feels* designed for a single-monitor setup, with its deeply connected panels that slide around each other. Nonetheless, it's convenient to use a multimonitor configuration, one in which you can divide windows, panels, and tools across different monitors to better support your workflow and organization. Thankfully, Blender supports multiple monitors, although it's not at first sight obvious *how*. To work with multiple monitors, start by clicking and dragging an interface panel from its corner handle, holding down the *Shift* key as you do so. ▶1.29

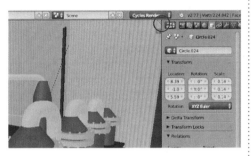

1.29

After you *Shift*-click the panel's corner handle, the panel detaches from the main interface as a free-floating window that can be dragged around. Using this technique for any panels, you can easily click and drag panels across multiple monitors, arranging the interface as needed. ▶1.30

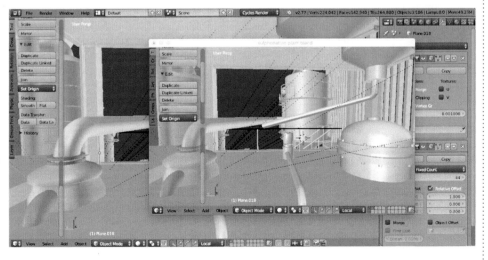

1.30

1.31

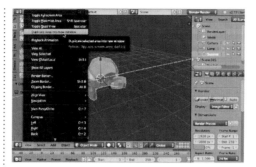

You can also access the same detachment feature by choosing *View > Duplicate Area into New Window* from the panel menu. ▶1.31

1.9 First-Person Controls

If you're modeling large environments, and especially first-person game environments, then it's useful to view the environment in first-person mode—that is, from the eye point of a potential character walking around within the environment, as opposed to at a distance, from the perspective of an artist or designer. You can easily activate first-person controls using the command *View > Navigation > Walk Navigation* from the 3D view menu. ▶1.32

1.32

After the first-person mode is activated, you can walk around by using the arrow keys or WASD keys on the keyboard. You can also move the mouse to orbit the head and look in different directions.

1.10 Align Camera to Viewport

Navigating the viewport is the most common task in Blender. And sometimes you come across an angle or perspective on the scene that looks simply fantastic; it's just what you need for your camera! In fact, it'd be great if you could simply align a camera to the viewport angle, allowing you to save your ideal view of the scene. Well, you can! To achieve this, start by positioning your viewport to find a view you want to save. ►1.33

1.33

After positioning the viewport, select *View > Align View > Align Active Camera to View* from the 3D view menu. ►1.34

1.34

When you select this option, the active camera aligns itself to match the angle of the viewport. If the scene has only one camera, it automatically becomes the "active camera." If your scene has multiple cameras, you can make any camera "active" by first selecting the camera and then choosing *View > Cameras > Set Active Object as Camera* from the 3D view menu. ►1.35

1.35

1.36

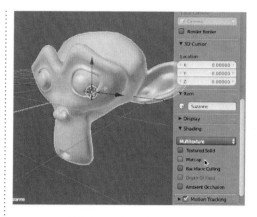

1.37

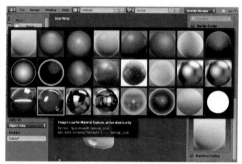

1.38

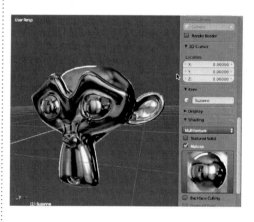

1.11 *MatCap*

When sculpting or modeling complex meshes, especially organic meshes, it's helpful to preview the mesh under real-time lighting, seeing how its curves and topology react to the environment. This makes the modeling process more intuitive for artists. One way to achieve realistic real-time previews for mesh materials is to configure the 3D viewport into rendered mode. This can sometimes be slow and computationally expensive. Another, more economical and efficient method is to enable the *MatCap* feature (short for *Material Capture*). When enabled, you can easily and quickly achieve real-time lighting and shading previews for your meshes during the modeling phase. To enable *MatCap*, expand the N Panel, and click the *MatCap* check box. ▶1.36

Once enabled, the shading of models in the 3D viewport changes into *MatCap* mode, and the *MatCap* selection button appears in the N Panel, allowing you to choose between different shading styles. Click the *Styles* drop-down menu, and select a style that works best for your purposes. ▶1.37

MatCap is a highly useful shading model for quickly previewing a mesh surface, complete with shading and reflections. ▶1.38

1.12 Text Editing

When working in teams, sharing assets and files between many members, you'll frequently need to annotate and communicate your intentions with others. One way to do this effectively in Blender is to write notes and comments directly in the Blender file. These can be viewed by others. To achieve this, you can use the *Text Editor* window, which is a long-standing but lesser-known feature. To access the *Text Editor* window, click on the mode dropdown list inside any panel, and then choose the *Text Editor* option. ▶1.39

To create a new text file, click the *New* button from the tool bar. After clicking this button, you can type text into the text editor. Unfortunately, Blender does not currently support rich text formatting, as well as alternative fonts and formatting, such as bold, italic, and others. ▶1.40

You can access additional text editing options (e.g., text size, text searching, and find-and-replace functionality) from the *Text Editor* tools panel. The tools panel can be seen by selecting *View > Properties* from the text editor menu. ▶1.41

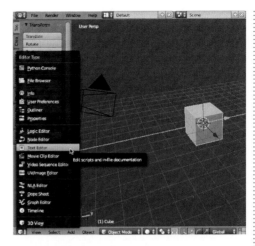

1.39

1.40

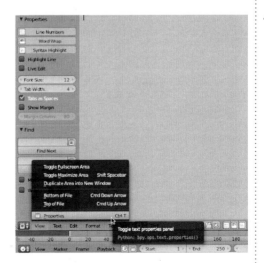

1.41

1 Interface Cheats

1.13 Scroll Editing

There are many ways to edit an object's properties—such as position, rotation, and scale. You can use the transform gizmo in combination with the mouse and keyboard shortcut keys, and you can also type values directly into the text fields from the N Panel and Properties panel. These editing methods work well in almost all cases. ▶1.42

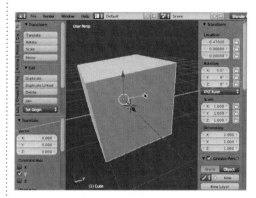

1.42

However, there's another method for editing properties that can work very quickly and intuitively, especially on a selection of mice with auto-roll functionality for the middle mouse wheel, like the Logitech Performance MX mouse. Using this method, you can hover your mouse cursor over any numerical text box, holding down the *Ctrl* key on the keyboard and rolling the middle mouse wheel up or down to raise or lower the property, respectively. ▶1.43

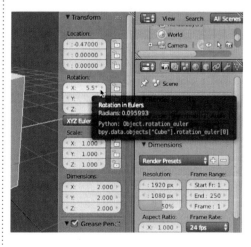

1.43

1.14 Hide the Splash Screen

1.44

By default, Blender is configured to display the splash screen on start-up—that is, the welcome window, which displays a Blender render from the community, as well as offering access to recently opened files and other resources. This window can sometimes be helpful and informative, but for many seasoned users it simply gets in the way. It becomes the kind of window that you simply close every time. ▶**1.44**

1.45

Thankfully, you can hide the splash screen, preventing it from popping up every time Blender starts! To achieve this, access the *User Preferences* window by choosing *File > User Preferences* from the application menu.
Then from the *Interface* tab, remove the check mark from the *Show Splash* check box. ▶**1.45**

NOTE

Don't forget to save the user preferences after changing them.

1.46

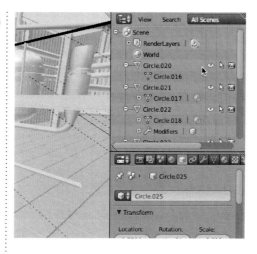

1.47

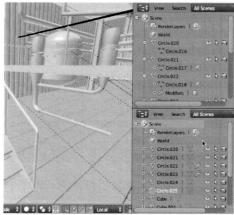

1.15 Dual Outliners

The Outliner window lists all objects in the scene in a hierarchical way, representing the parent–child relationship between objects. Most of the time, just one Outliner is all you'll need for selecting, renaming, and rearranging objects. ▶1.46

For large scenes with many objects (perhaps hundreds or even thousands), however, it's useful to have two Outliner windows side by side or one above the other. Using this arrangement is useful for parenting different objects to another object. You can use one Outliner to view the parent and the other Outliner to drag and drop the children to the parent, dragging and dropping between the two Outliners. ▶1.47

1.16 Viewport Visibility

You'll frequently want to customize and change what you see in the 3D viewport. Sometimes, this will be to limit the number of visible objects, allowing you to concentrate more on a particular task—like modeling. And sometimes this will be to get a better preview of what will actually be rendered. What follows are some of the critical ways in which you can customize viewport rendering and visibility.

1.16.1 Viewport Background

By default, the Blender 3D viewport features a solid-shaded background—just one color (gray) filled throughout. This background is neutral, low contrast, and subtle, which is a good choice because it's easier for you to concentrate on your work. But sometimes a single bold color can run against your workflow, especially if your objects, materials, and scene closely resemble the background color itself. Thankfully, Blender lets you customize the background color. To achieve this, access the *User Preferences* window by selecting *File > User Preferences* from the application menu. From here, activate the *Themes* tab, and then choose *3D View* from the list. ▶1.48

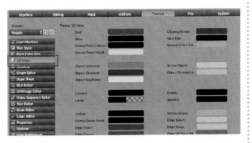

1.48

After accessing the 3D view interface settings, scroll down the page to the *Gradient High/Off* color swatch. This controls the bold color to be used for the viewport background. You can pick a different color to change the background. ▶1.49

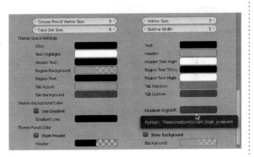

1.49

You can also apply a gradient fill to the background, transitioning between two colors, one at the top of the viewport moving toward the one at the bottom. You apply a gradient, enable the *Use Gradient* check box, and select the second color from the *Gradient Low* field. ▶1.50

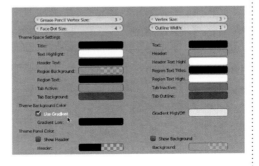

1.50

1.51

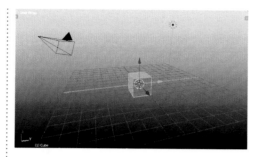

A gradient fill to the viewport, when applied using complementary colors, can add an important dynamism and interest to the scene for the modeler. It can enhance your workflow and make it easier to preview colors and materials. ▶1.51

1.52

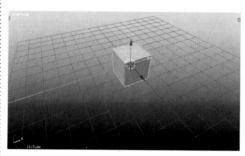

1.16.2 Viewing Axes and the Grid

Every new scene in Blender displays the floor grid and axis guidelines. The floor grid is simply a grid of equally spaced cells spanning the extents of the scene floor. The axis guidelines instead represent color-coded world axes (lines) for X, Y, and Z. These together make it easier to orient yourself inside the viewport regardless of your viewing angle. They are also highly useful for object snapping, for moving and positioning objects by discrete increments. ▶1.52

1.53

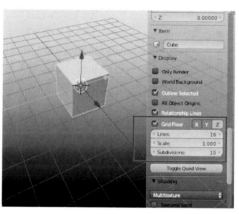

You toggle the visibility of both the floor grid and the axes from the *Display* section of the N Panel. Remove the check mark from the *Grid Floor* check box to disable the floor grid. And click the X, Y, and Z buttons to toggle the visibility of the world axes. ▶1.53

1.16.3 Global and Local Views

When creating large environments, it's easy for the 3D viewport to fill with objects and meshes and other props. When this happens, it gets harder to work and concentrate on single, specific objects. Other views, angles, and objects can interrupt your view. This is where Blender's Local/Global View comes in very handy! By default, the viewport is in Global View, allowing you to see all objects that have not been manually hidden from the Outliner view. ▶1.54

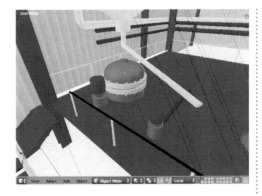

1.54

Local View, in contrast, temporarily hides all objects, except for the selected objects. This allows you to see only the selected objects in isolation. To access Local View, click *View > View Global/Local* from the 3D view menu. You can deactivate this mode by selecting the same option again—it can be toggled. ▶1.55

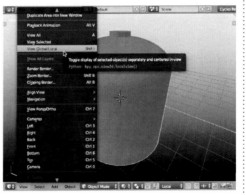

1.55

1.16.4 Showing Rendered Objects

While building a scene, it's common to make objects that'll never be rendered: lamps, empty objects, image planes, particle systems, splines, cameras, and even meshes that are hidden in some frames during an animation. This is a reasonable workflow, but sometimes you'll want the viewport to display only the objects that will be rendered. You can achieve this easily by opening the N Panel and, from the *Display* section, choosing the option *Only Render*. ▶1.56

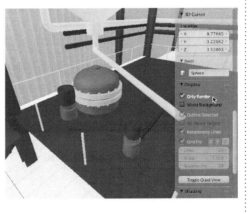

1.56

2

Selections

When asked to list Blender's best features, most people ignore selection techniques. Selecting objects isn't exactly a sexy or exciting topic. Most people take it for granted. This is probably because selection is never an end in itself; it's always a means to an end. Selecting objects is something you do on the way to producing something else. But without the ability to select objects and parts of objects, very little could ever be achieved in Blender. More than this, making selections is something you do frequently! Thus, selecting is a critical activity, and the speed at which selections are made dramatically affects how quickly things get done in the long term. For this reason, let's take time out to see some tips and tricks for selecting stuff!

2 Selections

2.1 *Edit* Selection Modes

Edit mode is accessed either by pressing *Tab* on the keyboard or by switching to *Edit* mode from the *Mode* drop-down list on the 3D view toolbar. *Edit* mode

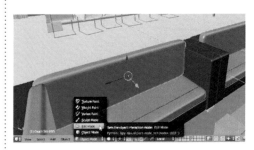

allows you to access and change the constituent pieces of mesh—namely its vertices, edges, and faces. You probably knew that already. ▶2.1

While in *Edit* mode, the selection is restricted by the Selection Filter. With the *Faces Filter* activated, you can select faces, the *Vertex Filter* for vertices, and the *Edge Filter* for edges. ▶2.2

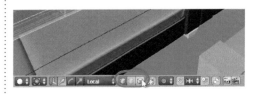

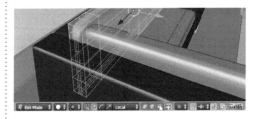

However, you're not restricted to selecting just one kind of thing at a time. You can select vertices, edges, and faces *together*, without having to switch between selection modes. To do this, hold down the *Shift* key on the keyboard while clicking the filter mode icons from the 3D view toolbar. Clicking each button expands the Selection Filter, across vertices, edges, and faces. ▶2.3

2.2 Layers and Selections

You'll often need to select many objects in a scene. Sometimes this will be to hide or show objects, or perhaps to delete objects, or even to move objects in one operation. Furthermore, you'll need to select the *same group* of objects *many times*. This normally happens when you move, edit, or change objects and then later decide to change them back or tweak them further. One way to achieve multiobject selection is to hold down the *Shift* key on your keyboard and click each object to select exactly the ones you need. ▶2.4

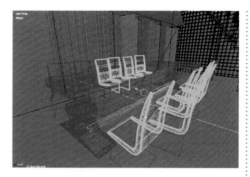

2.4

The problem, however, is that this can be time-consuming and tedious if there are many objects, and especially so if the objects are scattered all over the scene! You'd have to pick an object, move the viewport some more, pick another object, and so on—which is boring. A more promising solution, then, is to be found in *Layers*, which are accessed from the 3D view toolbar, provided the view is not in *Local* mode (see Chapter 1). ▶2.5

2.5

Layers let you collect multiple objects together, making it easier to view and select them and to reselect them. When objects are assigned to the *same* layer, they can be viewed together in isolation, separate from everything else. This lets you easily focus on only the objects you need. To assign the selected objects to a layer, start by choosing *Object > Move to Layer* from the 3D view menu (or press *M* on the keyboard). ▶2.6

2.6

Now you'll see the *Layer Picker* menu. From here, click on a layer slot to move the selected objects to the destination layer. If the destination layer (the layer your objects are moving to) is different from the currently active layer (the layer you're currently viewing), then the selected objects will disappear after moving to the destination layer. ▶2.7

2.7

2 Selections

2.8

2.9

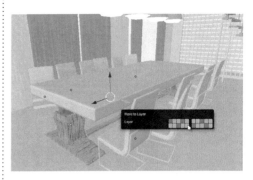

2.10

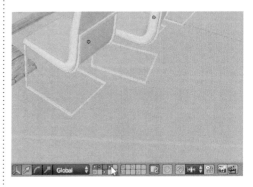

You can view the contents of any layer in the viewport simply by clicking on the corresponding layer button, from the 3D view toolbar. Layers containing a dot icon have objects assigned to them, whereas undotted layers are empty and contain no objects. ▶2.8

When you pick a *single* layer, only the objects on that layer become visible in the viewport, and all other objects disappear. You can assign the same objects to *multiple* layers, and you can view multiple layers *at the same time*. To assign the selected objects to multiple layers, simply hold down the *Shift* key on the *Layer Picker* menu, which appears after choosing *Object > Move to Layer* from the 3D view menu. ▶2.9

You can view multiple layers at the same time by clicking *Ctrl+* on each layer from the *Layer Visibility* buttons, on the 3D View toolbar. ▶2.10

NOTE

If you need to remove objects from layers after assignment, you can either reassign them to a completely new and single layer or toggle-assign them by *Shift*-clicking on the layer from which you want to remove them, via the *Layer Picker* menu.

2.3 Layer Management

While layers are a great way to group and organize objects, they'd be even better if Blender let us customize them further. It'd be great if we could name layers, select all objects on a layer, toggle layer visibility more intuitively, and even create layer groups that can be hidden and shown together in one operation. We can achieve these by using the *Layer Management* add-on. To install this, access the *User Preferences* window, and select the *Add-ons* tab. From here, type "layer management" into the search field at the top left-hand side of the window, and then Enable the *Layer Management* add-on option to enable the add-on. ▶2.11

2.11

When *Layer Management* add-on is enabled, a new tab, *Layers*, will have been added to the 3D view toolbar, at the left-hand side of the window. This tab is available only in Object mode. It is divided into two sections, *Layer Management* and *Layer Groups*. From the *Layer Management* tab, you can hide, show, rename, and organize layers. From the *Layer Groups* tab, you can hide and show multiple layers in one operation by grouping layers together. ▶2.12

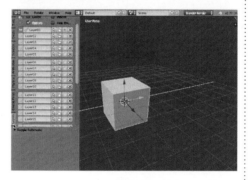

2.12

From the *Layer Management* section (of the *Layers* tab), you can assign each layer a descriptive and meaningful name by typing a name into its text edit field. Using the *Layer* buttons, you can *select* or *deselect* all objects on a layer, lock or unlock all objects (preventing them from being selected), and even toggle their visibility as well as their viewport appearance (solid or wireframe display). ▶2.13

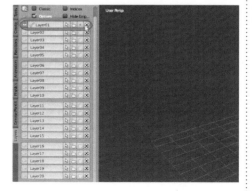

2.13

2 Selections

2.14

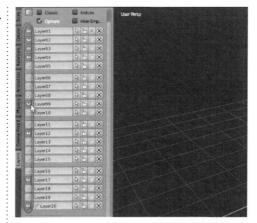

The *Layer Groups* section is especially useful for quickly hiding or showing specific combinations of layers. To use this feature, first select a combination of layers from the *Layer Management* tab by clicking the eye icon for each layer you select. ▶2.14

2.15

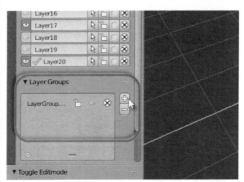

Then, to save the selected combination, click the + button from the *Layer Groups* tab, to add a new group for the active combination. ▶2.15

2.16

NOTE

Removing a layer group does not delete or remove the associated layers.

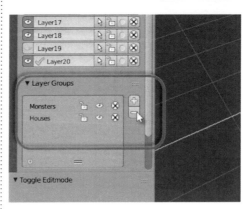

After creating a layer group, you can hide or show all layers belonging to the group, lock them, change their display mode, and remove the group itself. ▶2.16

2.4 Groups

In addition to *Layers*, Blender offers *Groups* for quickly selecting multiple objects in a scene. Groups are unrelated to and separate from layers. Groups are ideal for selecting multiple objects in the viewport as though they were a single, combined mesh. To start using groups, select multiple objects in the scene that belong together or should be edited as one—just as though you were going to assign them to a layer. ▶2.17

2.17

2.18

To assign the selected objects to a group, choose *Object > Group > Create New Group* from the 3D view menu, or press the associated keyboard shortcut (*Ctrl + G*). ▶2.18

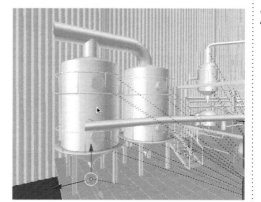

2.19

After creating a new group, the outline for the selected objects will automatically change to green in the viewport. A green outline indicates that the selected objects are part of a group. ▶2.19

Once you've made a group, you'll probably want to name it meaningfully and also be able to select it (and all objects in the group) quickly. To do this, you can use the Outliner window. From the Outliner window, change the filter type to *Groups* using the *Filter* drop-down list. On selecting this option, the Outliner window displays only the groups in the scene,

2.20

and it also lists all child objects belonging to the group, making it easier to view and select groups. ▶2.20

2.21

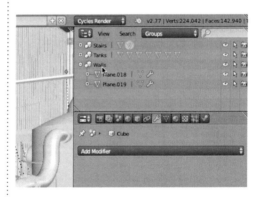

To select a group, just click its name in the Outliner window, and all objects belonging to the group are automatically selected too. When they are selected, you can *Translate*, *Rotate*, and *Scale* the group (as well as all objects within it) just like a regular mesh. You can also expand the group in the Outliner and select specific objects within the group individually. ▶2.21

2.22

To rename a group, double-click its name inside the Outliner, and then enter a new name. You can also hide or show all objects in the group by toggling the group's visibility icon (eye icon) beside its name within the Outliner. ▶2.22

2.5 Vertex Groups

The selection methods considered hitherto focus on selecting one or more *objects* in the scene—specifically, complete and whole objects, like buildings, characters, weapons, and others. But when working in *Edit* mode, you'll frequently need to select *parts* of a *single object*, such as the hood of a car mesh, the trunk of a tree, or the nose in a head. These parts are simply collections of vertices, edges, and faces; and they can be very time-consuming to select. In *Edit* mode therefore, you'll want features for remembering combinations of vertices (just like *Layers* and *Groups* for objects) to help quickly select and reselect specific combinations at the touch of a button. One method for achieving this is vertex groups. A vertex group, simply stated, represents a saved selection of vertices within a mesh. To get started at using vertex groups, a new vertex group must be created. Select a mesh for which a group should be made, and switch to the *Object Data* tab from the *Properties* window. From here, you can view the *Vertex Groups* list, which lists all vertex groups associated with the mesh. By default, a mesh has no vertex groups. ▶2.23

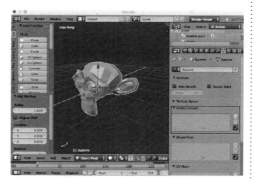

2.23

To create a new vertex group, click the + button from the *Vertex Groups* list. After creation, the vertex group begins in empty state; that is, it contains no associated vertices. Before adding vertices, name the group appropriately—just by double-clicking the vertex group name from the list and then entering a new name, such as ear, branch, handle, or whatever is suitable. ▶2.24

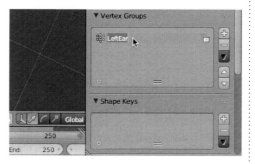

2.24

2.25

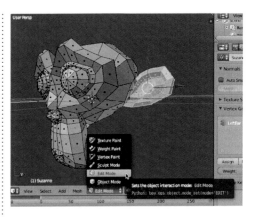

To start adding a selection of vertices to the group, enter *Edit* mode for the object, and then select all the vertices to add. That is, select all the vertices *whose selection* you want Blender to remember. ▶2.25

While in *Edit* mode, and with the vertices selected, click the *Assign* button from the *Vertex Groups* list in the Properties panel to assign the selected vertices to the active vertex group. Assigning the vertices does not change their structure or connectivity within the mesh in any way but only stores the selection. ▶2.26

After vertices are assigned to the group, you can easily select them by first choosing the appropriate vertex group from the list and then choosing the *Select* button from the Properties panel in the *Object Data* tab. This selects all vertices in the mesh associated with the active group. Easy! Just a one-click operation for selecting many vertices. ▶2.27

2.26

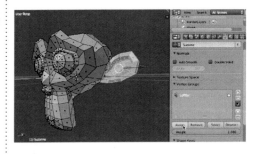

2.27

2.6 Selecting NGons

The selection techniques considered so far assume you already know what you need to select, whether objects or polygons. But sometimes you just need to make specific kinds of selections based on *criteria*, and you don't know in advance which objects satisfy those criteria. A common example is selecting all NGons in a mesh—that is, all faces with more than four sides. NGons are generally bad for game engine models and models that must be animated or subdivided. For this reason, modelers and animators strive to remove NGons from models. Hence, it's important to find, select, and address all NGons quickly and efficiently. In simple models, it's easy to find and remove NGons. However, the issue becomes troublesome for complex models with many faces and polygons. In these models, NGons are not so clearly visible, and you'll need Blender to help you find them. ▶2.28

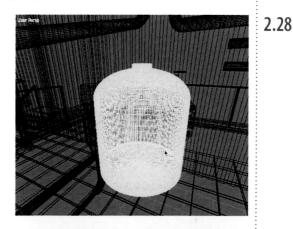

2.28

2.29

Blender lets you select all faces in the model by the number of sides. To achieve this, select the model, and enter *Edit* mode. Then choose *Select > Select All by Trait > Select Faces by Sides.* ▶2.29

On choosing this option, some faces in the selected mesh may be automatically selected. You can control which faces are selected by using the settings presented in the Tools panel, from the *Select Faces by Sides* field. To find all NGons, change the *Type* field to *Greater Than* and the *Number of Vertices* field to *4*, and then remove the check mark from the *Extend* field. The *Extend* check box,

2.30

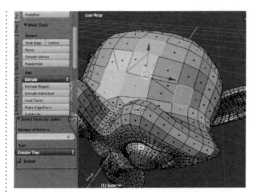

if enabled, leaves the current selection unchanged and simply adds (*extends*) to it. ▶2.30

2.31

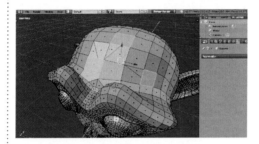

Once the NGons search settings are specified, all NGons in the mesh are selected. You can easily check how many faces and vertices were selected by reading from the info panel. ▶2.31

2.32

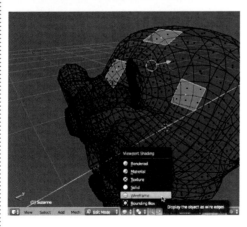

On complex meshes, with many curves, holes, and recesses, it can sometimes be difficult to spot all NGons, even when they're selected. To help improve the visibility of the selected faces, you can switch viewport shading to *Wireframe* mode by using the *Shading* drop-down list from the 3D view toolbar. ▶2.32

2.7 Edge Loops and Shortest Path Selections

When modeling complex objects (e.g., organic models), you'll often need to select an edge loop—that is, a set of connected edges running sequentially in a line across the surface of a model. Sometimes you'll need a *complete* edge loop, but other times you'll need only a fraction of it. To select a complete edge loop in *Edit* mode, select just one edge from the model, and then choose *Select > Edge Loops* from the 3D view menu. This selects the complete edge loop, which passes through the selected edge. ▶2.33

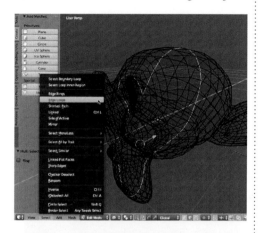

2.33

Sometimes you don't want to select a complete edge loop but only a fraction of it. This is useful when, for example, you want to select only the front edges of a loop running vertically along a character's face, as opposed to all edges running around the back. Blender can do this too! To achieve partial selection, choose the first and last edges of the edge loop that you need, and then choose *Select > Shortest Path* from the 3D view menu. Doing this selects all edges running on the shortest path between the two selected end edges. This works also for edges that aren't in the same edge loop, but selecting edges within the same edge loop often makes the most sense. ▶2.34

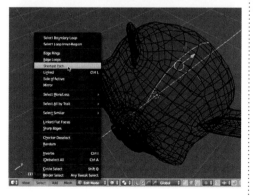

2.34

2.35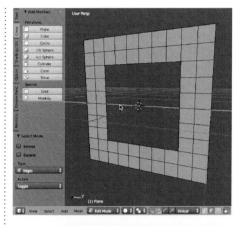

2.8 Selecting Perimeter Edges

Imagine this scenario. You create a plane object in the scene to act as a wall for an interior environment. Then you cut a square hole into it for a window opening looking outside. Having done this, you need to select all edges running around the window hole, to create a frame and a ledge. ▶2.35

2.36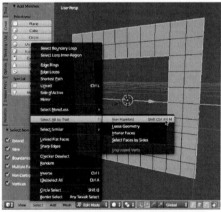

Now maybe you could select all the perimeter edges by clicking each one or, in some cases, by dragging a rectangle selection over them. But sometimes the edges may not be so easily selectable, or maybe there are just too many edges! This is where *Non Manifold* selection comes to the rescue. Simply click *Select > Select All by Trait > Non Manifold* from the 3D view menu. ▶2.36

2.37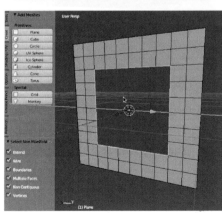

Choosing this option selects *all* the perimeter edges in the mesh—that is, all edges connected to only one face. This may select some unintended edges, so you may have to deselect some edges to get exactly the selection you need. ▶2.37

2.9 Selecting UV Seams and Linked Selection

When mapping complex objects (from heads to cars), you'll typically lay out the UVs into separate and distinct islands, using either manual methods like Mark Seam or automatic methods like Smart UV Project. Whichever way you go, UV mapping effectively inserts dummy cuts or spices into the model along the edges (UV seams), allowing the mesh topology to flatten out into a 2D space. In principle, this divides the mesh faces into separate areas, corresponding to the UV islands. ▶2.38

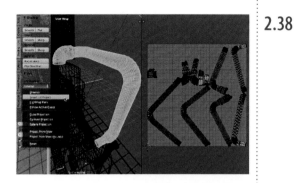

2.38

It's often helpful, while modeling and mapping, to select all faces in each island—for tweaking or adjustment. You can do this easily and quickly just by selecting only one face in an island inside the 3D viewport and then choosing *Select > Linked* from the menu. ▶2.39

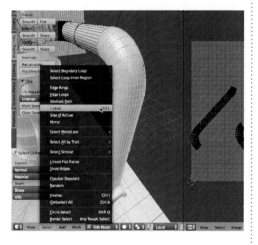

2.39

When choosing *Select > Linked* while in *Face* mode, the selection repeatedly expands outward from the selected face, and the selection stops only when a delimiting edge or condition is found. You can choose which kind of edge or condition should act as the delimiter. The delimiter is that which stops the selection expansion. You can pick this by using the Tools panel.

2.40

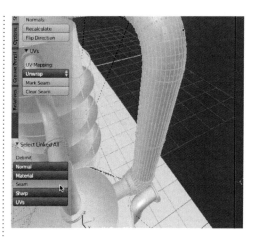

When the delimiter is a UV seam, then all faces on a UV island can be selected in one click or keyboard shortcut. Powerful selection technique! ▶2.40

2.10 Selecting Objects from Patterns

It sometimes happens that your scene gets messy. You end up with many objects named Cube01, Cube02, and Sphere02, or something similar. There's no obvious structure or hierarchy to your objects, and the object names don't properly express what they're intended for. This kind of situation is far from ideal, but it's almost an inevitable part of working in 3D, whether it's happened to your own projects or to an inherited project you need to work on. ▶2.41

2.41

When you get a messy scene, like the one described, you'll need to develop some new working strategies. A common task is to select all objects of a common type—all cubes or all spheres or cones—without having to manually find and click each one. If the objects all have similar names or feature common words, then selecting them needn't be hard work. You can use the *Select Pattern* tool. Using this tool, you can easily select one or more objects according to a search criterion. To access *Select Pattern*, choose *Select > Select Pattern* from the 3D menu. ▶2.42

The *Select Pattern* tool displays a dialog allowing you to enter a search string (letters, numbers, and symbols) defining a criterion. Entering the word *Box* finds and selects all objects named *Box*. Entering the word **Box* finds and selects all objects with names including the word *Box*, but the selected objects may also have unspecified characters *before* the word *Box*, such as *BigBox*, *New Box*, and *001Box*. Entering the word **Box** selects objects whose names contain the word *Box*, regardless of prefixes and suffixes—such as *BigBox*, *BoxBig*, and *SuperBoxBig*. ▶2.43

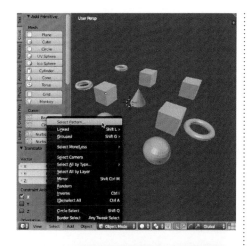

2.42

2.43

2.11 Random Selection

It might seem crazy, but Blender has a random selection option! If you choose *Select > Random* from the 3D view, Blender randomly selects some faces in the model. It will pick any number of faces, and none of them will be necessarily related. ▶2.44

From the Tools panel, you can customize the selection options.

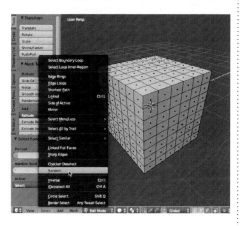

2.44

2.45

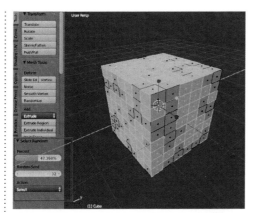

By default, the *Action* mode is set to *Select*, which means that faces in the model are selected. The action can be *Deselect* instead, which can be used to deselect faces. The *Percent* field caps the maximum number of faces that can possibly be selected in the model. And the *Random Seed* field can be scrolled through to pick a different set of faces each time. ▶**2.45**

2.46

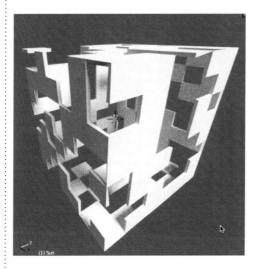

The random selection tool may initially seem useless, but actually it's useful for creating a patterned and abstract act, as well as adding noise and deformations to a model, and also for scattering debris and rubble across a terrain, among others. ▶**2.46**

2.12 Selection and Visibility

Blender has many automated selection methods, including *Select Random*, *Select Pattern*, *Select Similar*, and others. These require you to define a search criterion, and then Blender indiscriminately selects faces from among *all* faces in the model according to that criterion. Often, however, you'll want to be pickier. You'll want to restrict the faces through which Blender searches and selects. Rather than search for *all* faces, you'll want to search through only a *fraction* of them. This not only saves time but also limits the faces that can get affected—such as selecting random faces only on a character's forehead, without selecting them from elsewhere, like the nose, ear, or chin. To achieve this kind of filtering, you can use the *Hide* and *Show* face functionality. Specifically, by hiding all the faces to be discounted from the search, Blender will restrict its search to only visible faces. For example, consider 2.47, in which randomly selected faces have been extruded upward. ▶2.47

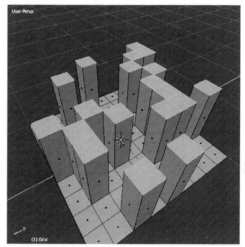

2.47

The model in 2.47 could easily become the basis for a cityscape scene, with many high-rise tower offices and skyscrapers. But the height of each building should be adjusted to make the scene more believable, as some buildings are taller than others. To do this, we can randomly select some rooftops and then lower or raise them. In this case, however, we only want to select random faces *among the rooftops*, not faces from the ground or side of buildings. Therefore, before using *Select Random*, we should hide all the faces to exclude from the selection. To do this, select the rooftop faces by picking one, and then choose *Select > Select Similar > Co-planar* from the 3D menu. This selects all the other rooftop faces, as these exist on the same plane. ▶2.48

2.48

2.49

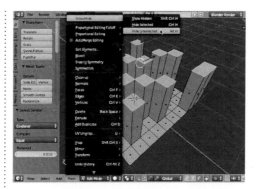

Having made a selection of the critical rooftop faces, let's hide the rest. To hide the unselected faces, choose *Mesh > Show/Hide > Hide Unselected* from the 3D view menu. This hides all the unselected faces, including those on the ground and the building walls. ▶2.49

2.50

NOTE

To display hidden faces again, choose *Mesh > Show/Hide > Show Hidden* from the 3D view menu.

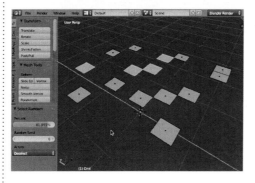

Now the viewport displays only the selected rooftop faces. If you now choose *Select > Random* from the 3D view menu, Blender will only apply the random selection to the visible faces, ensuring that any selected faces will always be rooftop faces! This is a great way of controlling selections. ▶2.50

2.51

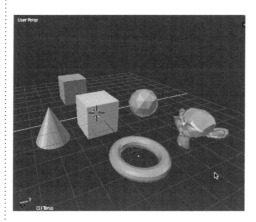

2.13 *Lasso* Selection

The *Lasso* selection tool lets you draw freehand a selection border around objects in the viewport, and objects included in the border are selected. This tool is especially used for selecting objects, carefully and precisely, that don't appear close together in the viewport but instead appear scattered around and between other objects that shouldn't be selected. ▶2.51

Interestingly, the *Lasso* tool doesn't have a menu option. It cannot be selected from the menu. It can, however, be accessed through a keyboard shortcut, which changes depending on the active control scheme being used. Thankfully, you can view the appropriate keyboard shortcut and even customize the control scheme through the *User Preferences* window. To get started, access the *User Preferences* window by choosing *File > User Preferences* from the application menu. ▶2.52

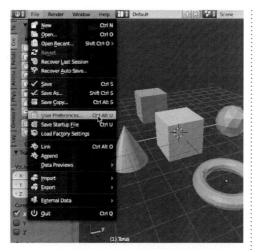

2.52

Next, activate the *Input* tab, and then enter the name *Lasso* into the *Name* field. This searches the active control scheme for the *Lasso* tool, finding all relevant keyboard and control bindings. ▶2.53

2.53

After the word *Lasso* is entered into the *Name* field, Blender finds all associated keyboard bindings. Scroll down to the *3D View* section, which affects controls for the 3D view, and expand a *Lasso* entry to view or define its keyboard shortcut. For the *Lasso* tool, I have used the shortcut *Alt + L*. ▶2.54

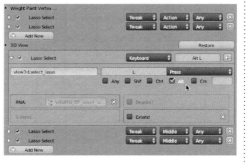

2.54

2.55

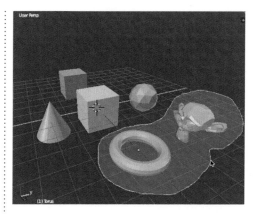

You can now access the *Lasso* tool using your chosen keyboard shortcut inside the 3D viewport. When active, simply move your mouse cursor inside the viewport to draw a border around the objects to select. Then click when you're done to confirm the border and select the objects. ▶**2.55**

2.56

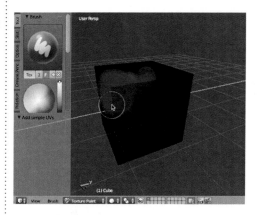

2.14 Selective Texture Painting

Texture Paint lets you paint pixels and textures onto your models directly from the 3D viewport using Photoshop-style brush tools. During the painting process, however, it's easy to make errors or slips where you accidentally paint onto the mesh on faces you never intended to paint, usually because of the viewport perspective or viewing angle. This happens whether you're using a mouse or a pen tablet. ▶**2.56**

2.57

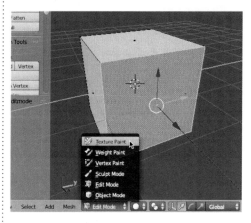

To protect against erroneous painting, you can use *Face Selection Masking.* This locks texture painting to only the selected faces. To achieve this, start by entering *Edit* mode, and select the faces for painting. Then switch over *to Texture Paint* mode. ▶**2.57**

When *Texture Paint* mode is active, enable the *Face Selection Masking* button from the 3D toolbar. When enabled, all texture painting is restricted to the selected faces. ▶2.58

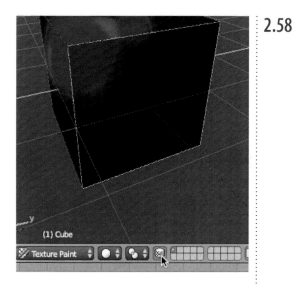

2.58

2.15 Vertex Weights and Selection

To see vertex weights in practice, let's try a sample project. You must create a house surrounded by a classical, green, wide lawn. On the lawn, grass grows abundantly, but there are some patchy areas where grass refuses to grow. This, then, is the problem: how to create a dense and grassy lawn from one mesh, with a mix of fertile and patchy areas. This problem need not be restricted to grassy lawns, of course; the same issue applies to balding heads, tattered clothes, stadiums full of dispersing people, and lots more. Let's start by creating a sample lawn from a plane object. Just create a *Grid* object in the scene, using the *Create* panel, and set the *X* and *Y* subdivisions to 16. ▶2.59

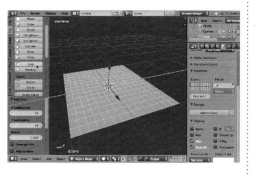

2.59

To define the areas of abundance and barrenness for the grass, we'll use vertex groups (discussed earlier in this chapter in Section 2.5). As mentioned, a vertex group represents a collection of vertices in the mesh. A group can be created manually using selection techniques, but it can also be created interactively using painting tools. And, as we'll see, vertex groups themselves represent selections. You can interactively paint a vertex group onto the selected mesh by entering *Weight Paint* mode, available from the 3D toolbar. ▶**2.60**

2.60

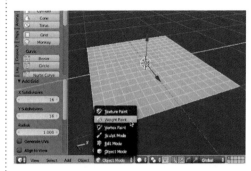

When in *Weight Paint* mode, you can use the Brush tool, with either the mouse or the pen tablet, to paint directly onto the mesh vertices. The brush *Weight* can be set from the tools panel. A weight of *0* is coded as blue and represents deselection, and a weight of *1* is coded as red and represents complete selection. Values between define midway values of selection. Using these tools, red areas represent grassy abundance, and blue represents grassy emptiness. These weight values have no *visible* qualities, of course. That is, they don't show in renders or animations or in textures; they simply encode selection values for vertices. ▶**2.61**

2.61

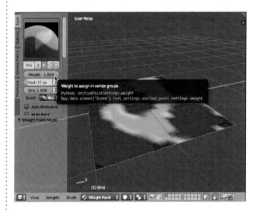

After painting weights in *Weight Paint* mode, switch to the *Object Data* tab for the mesh, inside the Properties panel. From there, a new vertex group will have been created and is listed in the *Vertex Groups* list. You should select this group and rename it appropriately. ▶**2.62**

2.62

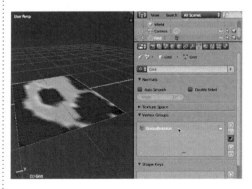

Now create the grass by adding a particle system in *Hair* mode. To do that, switch to the *ParticleSystem* tab for the mesh, from the Properties panel. Then click the + icon to add a new particle system onto the selected mesh. After this, select *Hair* for the *Type* drop-down field, to make the particle system emit hairs, which can simulate the effect of grass (specifically, green hairs!). ▶**2.63**

2.63

The grass hairs can be previewed from the viewport, stretching out of the mesh as gray lines. You can change the length and density of the hairs from the *Emission* tab, available in the Properties panel. Notice that, by default, hairs are generated across the mesh surface uniformly. ▶**2.64**

2.64

You can now configure the grass vertex group to influence the emission distribution of the hairs. In this case, the vertex group acts as a vertex selection, defining the emission surface. To achieve this,

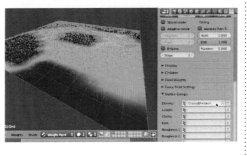

2.65

scroll down to the Properties panel, in the *Object Data* tab, to the *Vertex Groups* field. For the *Density* setting, specify the grass vertex group, the controlling field for the density. When you do this, the grass distribution changes across the mesh to match the vertex group selection. ▶**2.65**

And voila! You've just created a grassy field with a variable distribution of grass, based on a carefully painted selection of vertices, as defined by a vertex group. Behold the power of selections!

3

Modeling

Modeling is one of the most important activities in 3D. Simply put, it's the process of mesh building, whether you're modeling houses, cars, people, weapons, or anything else. Modeling is achieved through traditional *polygonal modeling* (with vertices, edges, and faces), as well as through *sculpting* workflows and image-based modeling (e.g., *displacement mapping*), as we'll see. This chapter focuses on tips and tricks in modeling and its related processes. However, given the extensive scope of the subject, there will inevitably be a lot left unsaid. This chapter includes some of the most useful, critical, and time-saving techniques for modeling. These are tips that stand apart in some important way—some because of the time and work they save you, others because of the convenience they offer, and still others because of the new perspectives and insights they can give you for working more effectively and productively. Let's see these tips and techniques in detail.

3 Modeling

3.1 Modeling from References

References are critically important raw material for modeling, especially during the initial phases. They include textures, photos, and concept art that act as inspiration and guidance for keeping your model on track. Blender offers many methods for importing reference material into the software so you can have it constantly visible and accessible during modeling. Perhaps the most intuitive and flexible method of import is through *Empty Objects*. To work with this method, create a new and empty object in the scene by switching to the *Create* tab in the 3D view and then clicking the *Empty* button. This creates an empty object in the scene. These are nonrenderable, diagnostic objects for the artist's benefit and use. ▶3.1

3.1

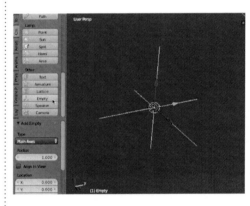

After creating and selecting the empty object, switch to the *Object Data* tab inside the *Properties* window, and change the *Display* type from *Plain Axis* to *Image*. This converts the empty object from a regular empty to one that holds images. ▶3.2

3.2

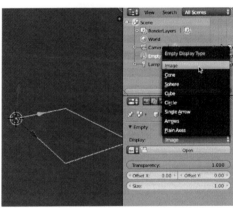

Next, click the *Open Image* button from the *Properties* window, and select a reference image from your hard drive. Once selected, the image is attached to the empty and appears in the viewport on a plane object. Excellent! You now have a reference image! Remember, the empty can be moved, scaled, and rotated with the transformation tools like any regular object. ▶3.3

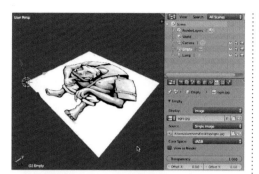

3.3

Let's now refine the image some more in the viewport, to better act as a reference rather than a distraction. Decrease the image *Transparency* setting, from the *Properties* window, to *0.2*. This makes the image less bold and partially transparent, allowing it to blend better with the scene. In addition, I often align the object pivot (origin) to the center of the image itself, as opposed to the default bottom-left corner. To do this, set the *Offset X* and *Y* to *–0.5*. ▶3.4

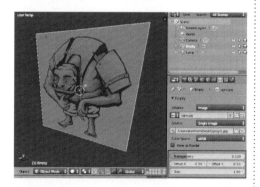

3.4

Last, you don't want to accidentally select, move, or edit the reference image while modeling. Its main purpose is just to be seen, viewed, and used as inspiration. So let's disable mouse picking using the Outliner. Just click the mouse cursor icon for the empty object. This prevents the object from being selected. And that's it: You have a nonselectable reference image! ▶3.5

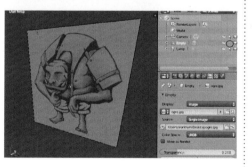

3.5

3 Modeling

3.2 Nondestructive Deformations

By activating *Edit* mode for the selected mesh, you can edit its vertices, edges, and faces, changing the mesh shape and structure. This is *polygonal modeling*, and it's a very powerful technique. However, it's a *destructive process* because once the mesh is remodeled in *Edit* mode, it can't easily be undone. That is, polygonal modeling can't be undone *unless* you manually remodel the mesh back to how it was. ▶3.6

3.6

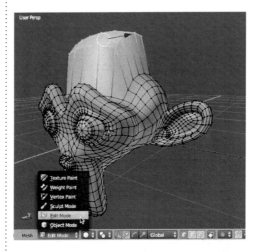

3.7

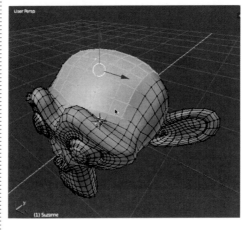

One way to get some *nondestructive* control over the form and shape of your mesh during modeling is to use *Hooks*. Hooks are special, independent objects that stick to groups of vertices in a mesh. They're used to push, pull, twist, and reshape the associated vertices. Admittedly, hooks can't extrude, bevel, or *add* any additional faces to a mesh—or *subtract*, but they're great for reshaping and changing existing vertices in a nondestructive way. Let's see how hooks work on a sample mesh. First, use *Edit* mode to grab some vertices, which should be sculpted or changed. ▶3.7

After selecting some vertices, create a new hook object. This will become a separate and independent object. It will be magnetized to the selected vertices and have influence over them. Moving the hook will move the associated vertices, and likewise for rotation and scaling. To create a new hook, select *Mesh > Vertices > Hooks > Hook to New Object* from the 3D view menu. ▶3.8

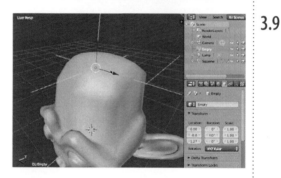

3.8

New hooks are created as empty objects and are listed in the Outliner. By transforming the hook (moving, rotating, or scaling), all associated vertices will transform with it. ▶3.9

By default, all associated vertices are fully magnetized to the hook object. Consequently, transforming the hook will transform all associated vertices equally and together. However, you can control a *soft selection* (or *falloff*) for the hook, allowing a differential weighting across the associated vertices. This lets a hook affect the vertices by different degrees, creating a soft and smooth deformation from the center moving outward. To control hook weighting, select the original mesh object, and view its modifiers from the *Modifiers* tab in the *Properties* window. ▶3.10

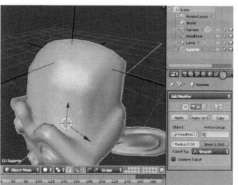

3.9

3.10

The hook modifier has been automatically added to the mesh, to establish the connection between its vertices and the hook. The hook modifier offers some settings to control hook weighting. The *Radius* field controls the extent of the hook's effect on the vertices: The higher this value, the more the vertices are affected. The *Strength* field is a master dial controlling the overall influence that a hook

3 Modeling

3.11

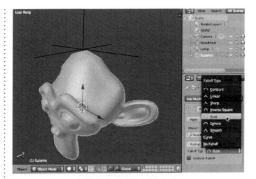

3.12

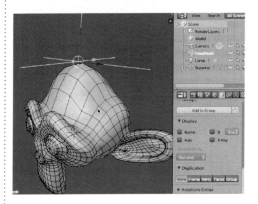

has over all associated vertices. And finally, the *Falloff Type* is a drop-down defining a curve controlling the shape and pattern of influence that the hook has over the associated vertices. By using a combination of these three parameters, a hook can create interesting and varied deformations. ▶**3.11**

Two exciting properties about hooks are that (1) they can be animated and (2) they are nondestructive. The latter makes sense because if a hook is deleted or the hook modifier is removed from the target mesh, then the influence of that hook (and its deformations) is subtracted from the mesh, as though the hook had never been created initially. ▶**3.12**

3.3 One-Sided Polygons

Most game engines, like Unreal and Unity, render polygons in a one-sided way for optimization reasons. That is, in game engines, polygons are only visible from one side; they are completely transparent from backside angles. When modeling for export to a games engine, therefore, it's useful to have Blender imitate an engine's approach to one-sided rendering, in order to better visualize how your models, characters, and environments will look in-engine. To achieve this, you should enable *Backface Culling*. To do that, expand the N Panel from the 3D view, and scroll down to the *Shading* section. From there, enable the option *Backface Culling.* ▶3.13

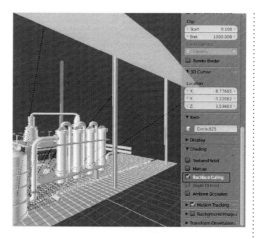

3.13

3.4 Duplication and "Multiple Modeling"

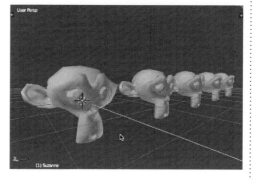

3.14

Take care, from a very early stage, about duplicating objects when modeling! Many objects eventually get repeated in a composition: pillars, trees, cogs, cars, distant buildings, pipes, tanks, windows, crowds of people, and more. Images and renders often contain many instances of them. Sometimes, these arrangements can be produced by a particle system—especially if they're animated—but many times you just need to duplicate meshes. ▶3.14

You can duplicate objects using the *Ctrl + D* keyboard shortcut or by using the 3D view menu: *Object > Duplicate Objects.* The limitations of this method, however, are twofold. First, each mesh duplicate is unique and occupies a substantial amount of system memory. This means that having many duplicates (especially high-poly duplicates) has a negative impact on the run-time performance of Blender. Second, the changes you make to one copy are not updated and propagated to the other copies because each copy is unique. For this reason, consider using the *Duplicate Linked* command. This can be accessed

3.15

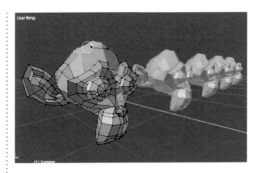

from the 3D view menu via *Object > Duplicate Linked*. Duplicating objects this way saves on system memory as all instances *share* the same object data. Plus, it allows edits and changes made to one instance to be reflected in all the other instances automatically. ▶3.15

3.5 Water, Waves, and Oceans

Creating oceans, seas, rivers, and reservoirs—and other bodies of moving water—is a common need. However, it poses many technical and artistic challenges. Thankfully, there are many ways to model water in Blender, and one of the simplest is the *Ocean* modifier. This modifier, when applied to *any* object, can create customizable, parametric waves that can be animated. And even if you

3.16

don't need an animation (e.g., when rendering a single frame), you can just pick the best frame from the animation. To get started, create an object in the scene (like a *grid*), and then switch to the *Modifiers* tab, from the *Properties* window. From there, add an *Ocean* modifier to the selected object. ▶3.16

3.17

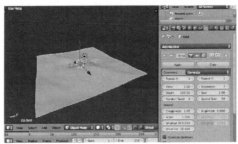

When an *Ocean* modifier is added to the selected object, an *Ocean* primitive mesh is automatically generated in the scene, replacing the original mesh. This is consistent with the *Ocean* modifier settings from the *Properties* window. By default, the *Generate* value is specified for the *Geometry* field. This can be left as is. ▶3.17

Next, let's animate the water across the timeline. Even if you don't need animated water, this is good practice. It gives you many frames from which you can select the best looking water. To do this, move the time slider to the first frame, inside the *Time Line* window, and then move your mouse cursor over the *Time* field for the water object, inside the Properties panel. Insert a key frame for this field (press *I*), locking down the value of the *Time* field for the first key frame. ▶3.18

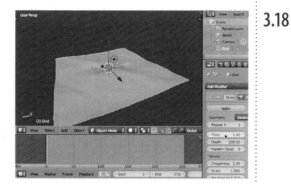

3.18

Move to the last frame, change the *Time* field to *10*, and then insert a key frame. This assigns a time value for the first and last frames, and now you have an animation for the water. This can be previewed in the 3D viewport either by pressing *Play* from the *Time Line* window or by clicking and dragging the time slider across the length of the timeline. ▶3.19

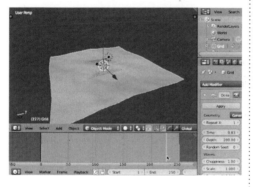

3.19

Finally, to improve the water's appearance, for realism or drama, you'll need to tweak some values from the *Ocean* modifier in the *Properties* window. Specifically, *Choppiness* controls the sharpness of the wave peaks: Higher values produce sharper and narrower peaks, simulating rougher waters. The *Scale* value controls the height and bumpiness of the water: Higher values increase the bumpiness. And the *Resolution* setting controls the detail of the water: Values beyond 10 produce very dense and performance-intensive water. Spend some time playing around with values. Note that if *Choppiness* and *Scale* are both very high, wave peaks often fold in on themselves and generate intersecting geometry, resulting in artifacts. For this reason, test run your water animation in the viewport to search for geometry intersections,

3.20

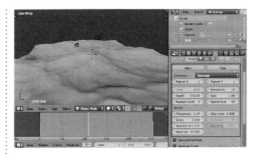

and correct them by adjusting the *Choppiness* and *Scale* values as needed. ▶3.20

3.6 Quads and Triangles

It's usually good practice to model only with *quads*, or *triangles*. NGons (polygons with more than four sides) are to be avoided for the problems they cause to game engines and subdivision surfaces. Sometimes when presented with a model featuring NGons, you'll want to convert the topology into quads and triangles. You can do this easily in Blender—first, by converting all faces into triangles, as every nontriangle face can, eventually, be converted into triangles. You can do this using the command *Mesh > Faces > Triangulate Faces* from the 3D menu. ▶3.21

3.21

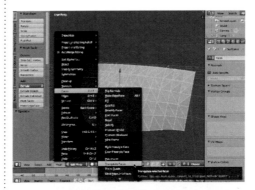

3.22

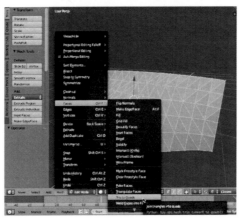

After your model is converted into triangles, you can convert the triangles into quads. (Some faces cannot be upscaled to quads because of their arrangement within the mesh, and thus they will remain as triangles.) To do this, select *Mesh > Faces > Tris to Quads*. ▶3.22

3.7 Bending

So you've modeled a long, straight mesh—like an interior corridor, a magic wand, or a flagpole—and now you need to bend it. ▶3.23

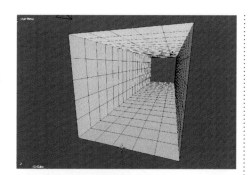

3.23

You can bend objects using the *SimpleDeform* modifier. When added, the modifier can be switched between different modes. Click the *Bend* button to access the bend functionality. ▶3.24

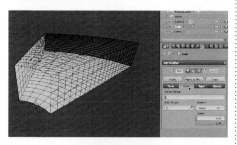

3.24

By default, your mesh may not bend on the intended axis. If so, it's not obvious how to change it, but you can do it. To change the bend direction, you'll need to create an empty object that will act as the *axis origin*. Start by creating a new empty object from the *Create* panel in the Tool Box. ▶3.25

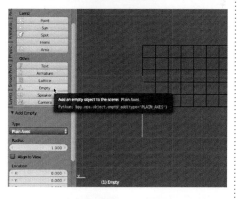

3.25

Next, link the bending object to the empty object through the *SimpleDeform* modifier, from the *Properties* window. Click the *Axis, Origin* field, and choose *Empty* from the drop-down list. This specifies the bend origin. ▶3.26

Having set the bend origin using the empty object, you can control the position and orientation of the bend by transforming the empty. This is a very powerful technique for applying the bend around any arbitrary axis!

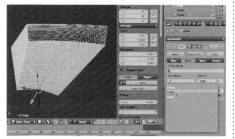

3.26

3.27

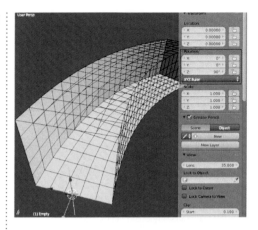

If the bend is following an unintended axis, then just rotate the empty. Remember, you can rotate the empty by precise angles using the N Panel type-in fields. ▶3.27

After you've established a bend axis using an empty, you can specify the bend angle with the *Angle* field, from the *Properties* window. Remember, the angle and bend only affect the mesh provided it has enough subdivisions—the mesh can only bend at the location of the vertices! ▶3.28

3.28

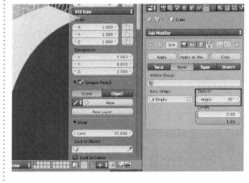

3.29

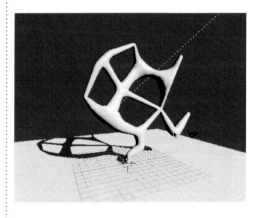

3.8 Meshes from Edges

If you need to make a tree, a system of pipes, a network of caverns, a modern art installation, a molecular structure, or any branching network of geometry, then consider the *Skin* modifier. It's great for quickly making branching thingies. It works by generating cubic geometry along every edge of a mesh, as though the edges represented extrusion paths. ▶3.29

The best way to get started is to make a box and then select all the vertices. Then choose *Mesh > Vertices > Merge* from the 3D menu, and choose *Merge at Center*. This reduces all the mesh vertices into one, consolidated vertex. This might seem a crazy thing to do—generating a mesh with one vertex—but it's actually a great starting point for the *Skin* modifier, as we'll see. ▶3.30

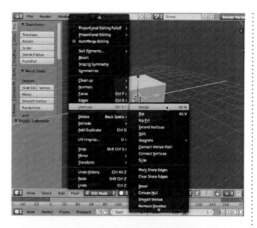

3.30

Next, apply the *Skin* modifier to the selected mesh, via the *Modifier* tab in the *Properties* window. This automatically generates some geometry around the single vertex. ▶3.31

3.31

From here, you can select the single vertex and extrude outward, using the *Extrude* button from the Tool Box. This creates a new vertex connected to the previous by a new edge. When this happens, the *Skin* modifier generates new geometry, extruding a cube along the edge as a path. You should repeat this process of vertex extrusion as needed to build the complete mesh network you need. ▶3.32

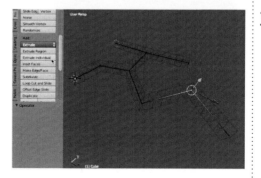

3.32

You can also *scale* the generated geometry at each vertex, using the *Skin Vertex Size* option. This assigns a weight to the vertices. It allows the generated geometry to be interpolated across the vertices, becoming smaller or larger, as defined by

3 Modeling

3.33

3.34

3.35

the scale for each vertex. Access to this option varies depending on the control scheme used. There is no direct menu entry (with one exception, which will be discussed shortly), and access is available via a keyboard shortcut only. However, only the Blender control scheme has a shortcut assigned by default (*Ctrl+A*). If you're using an alternative control scheme or a custom scheme, you'll need to define your own keyboard shortcut. To do that, access the Blender preferences using the *File > User Preferences* option from the file menu. ▶3.33

From the *User Preferences* window, select the *Input* tab to access the input options—a complete list of all keyboard/mouse shortcuts and controls for the application. Then expand the *3D View* group and then the *3D View (Global)* group. ▶3.34

Scroll to the bottom of the *3D View Global* list, and click the *Add New* button to add a new, custom keyboard shortcut. Then define the shortcut properties. I've used the shortcut *Alt + S*. Remember to click *Save User Settings* to confirm the settings and save them for continued use. ▶3.35

With the *Vertex Resize* option assigned to a keyboard shortcut, you can resize a vertex simply by selecting a vertex, pressing the designated keyboard shortcut, and then moving the mouse either up or down to increase or decrease the vertex size, respectively. ▶3.36

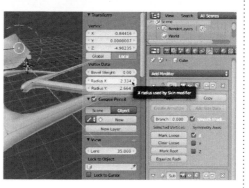

3.36

By default, the *Skin* modifier generates cubic geometry along the mesh edges, but you can add a *Subdivision Surface* modifier on top of the *Skin* modifier to smooth and round off the geometry. ▶3.37

3.37

Finally, although the *Skin Resize* option has no direct and obvious menu entry for resizing with the mouse, you can control the vertex size through two type-in fields for *Radius X* and *Radius Y* in the N Panel, which is available in *Edit* mode when the *Skin* modifier is applied. ▶3.38

3.38

3 Modeling

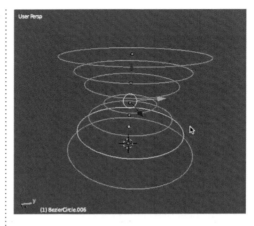

3.39

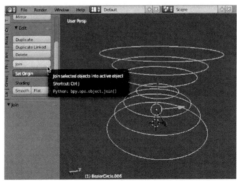

3.40

3.41

3.9 Spline Modeling

Did you know that you can build complete meshes from spline cross sections? That is, you can lay down a network of splines forming a wireframe cage, defining the surface of a mesh, and then Blender generates the mesh from the splines. This is an effective way of modeling smooth, hard surfaces like the body of a car, the shell of a rocket, or the body of a motorcycle. ▶3.39

To build a mesh from a spline network, simply create a sequence of closed splines. Then select them all. With all the splines selected, join them together into one spline, using the *Join* command from the Tools panel. ▶3.40

Next, convert the spline into a mesh. Select the spline, and from the 3D view menu, choose *Object > Convert to > Mesh from Curve*. This converts a curve type to a mesh type, providing access to all mesh editing options. When a curve is converted to a mesh, its control points become vertices and its line segments become edges. ▶3.41

After converting a curve sequence to a mesh, it remains only to generate faces between the new edge loops. To do this quickly and easily, you can use the *Loop Tools* add-on, which is great for automating many modeling tasks. To enable the add-on, access the *User Preferences* window by choosing *File > User Preferences* from the application menu. Then activate the *Add-ons* tab. From there, search for LoopTools, and enable the LoopTools option to activate the add-on. Be sure to click the *Save User Settings* button when completed. ▶3.42

3.42

Once you've activated *Loop Tools*, enter *Edit* mode for your newly converted mesh, and then select all edges through which the geometry should be generated. ▶3.43

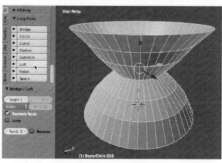

3.43

Next, expand the *Loop Tools* section of the *Create* tab, in the Tools panel, and click the *Loft* button. The *Loft* feature generates faces along the cross section of a sequence of closed edge loops. It is very powerful and can create faces quickly and easily across many splines! ▶3.44

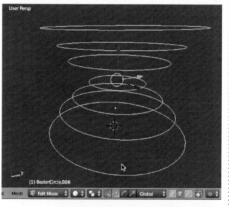

3.44

If your model ends up with thin, one-sided faces after the *Loft* operation, you can make the object thicker and two-sided using the *Solidify* modifier. And voila! A quick and easy way to generate complex geometry with two sides. ▶3.45

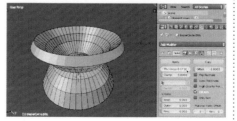

3.45

3 Modeling

3.10 Rebuilding Meshes: Retopology

High-poly modeling and sculpting allow for the creation of highly detailed models in 3D, complete with bumps, cracks, and microsurface details. Such details, however, necessarily require densely tessellated models. This can be technically problematic for game engines especially, as models and complex scenes perform poorly, unsurprisingly when burdened by the weight of millions of faces and vertices. To solve the problem, artists often retopologize models. That is, they convert a high-poly model into a low-poly version, using automated or semiautomated methods. The low-poly version features fewer polygons and details than its higher poly counterpart, but it can still display much of the microsurface detail from the high-poly version by using a *Normal Map*. A Normal Map is an image whose pixel data encode surface details, defining how a render system (e.g., *Cycles*) should shade the pixels of a face (in the low-poly model) to *simulate* the presence of surface detail where there isn't actually any. In any case, Blender offers several methods for generating a low-poly mesh from a high-poly mesh (*retopology*). Let's see some of them.

3.10.1 Decimation

Perhaps the simplest and "most automated" retopology system in Blender is the *Decimate* modifier. This lets you progressively generate lower poly versions of a mesh by simply tweaking a horizontal slider control from the *Properties* window. To add a *Decimate* modifier, select your mesh, and then switch to the *Modifiers* tab in the *Properties* window. From the *Modifiers* dropdown list, select the *Decimate* modifier. ▶3.46

3.46

Once added, the *Decimate* modifier offers controls for reducing mesh polygons. The *Ratio* field is a horizontal slider (and type-in field) defining the degree of fidelity to the original mesh. By default, *Ratio* is set to *1.0*, which means the original mesh is left unchanged. Lower values progressively reduce mesh polygons, though it always produces tris and quads. The *Faces* counter (shown at the bottom of the modifier) displays how many faces remain in the retopologized mesh, based on the *Ratio* setting. ▶3.47

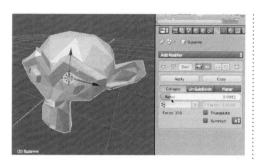

3.47

If you're happy with the result produced by *Decimate*, click *Apply* to bake the changes to the mesh, retaining them.

NOTE

Decimate destroys existing UVs, and it reduces polygons without any analysis of or consideration for edge flow. This means the resultant polygons and edge loops may be in any arrangement. This is potentially problematic for animation and subdivision, which depend on rigorous and ordered topology. For this reason, if you need to animate or subdivide your mesh, then *Decimate* (though easy to use) may not be for you.

3.10.2 *Shrink Wrap* Modifier

The *Shrink Wrap* modifier effectively takes two meshes as input, a high-poly mesh and a simpler, low-poly primitive (e.g., a cylinder). From these inputs, it automatically deforms the low-poly mesh to wrap around the contours of the high-poly mesh, just as the *Shrink Wrap* process deforms a plastic film around the shape of the wrapped object. ▶3.48

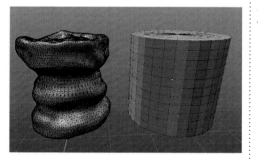

3.48

3.49

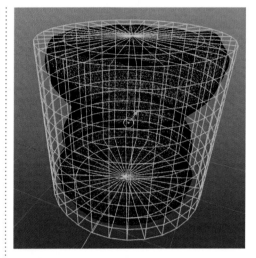

To use the *Shrink Wrap* modifier, position the low-poly mesh around the high-poly mesh. That is, adjust the low-poly mesh to completely surround and contain the high-poly mesh. Using the wireframe viewport display is often useful for achieving this. ▶3.49

3.50

Next, select the low-poly object, and from the *Properties* window, choose the *Modifiers* tab, and then add a *Shrinkwrap* modifier. ▶3.50

3.51

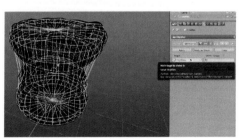

Finally, for the *Target* drop-down, select the *Target* (high poly) object. On choosing this, Blender automatically conforms the low-poly mesh to the high-poly mesh, effectively by snapping vertices in the source mesh to the nearest surface point in the target. ▶3.51

The modifier is continuously applied in *World Space*, not *Local Space*. This means that moving the low-poly mesh in the scene, even after the modifier is added, will affect the way it is shrink wrapped onto the high-poly mesh. You can bake the *Shrinkwrap* modifier by clicking the *Apply* button. This makes all mesh changes permanent. ▶3.52

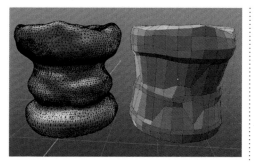

3.52

3.10.3 Surface Snapping

Surface snapping is, in short, a mostly manual method of shrink wrapping. Due to its manual nature, you get a lot of control over how a low-poly object conforms to a high-poly object. However, the process can also be slow and tedious. With Surface Snapping, Blender helps you move and position vertices in the low-poly mesh onto faces in the high-poly mesh, using snapping. As with shrink wrapping, you need to begin with a low-poly mesh and a high-poly mesh. ▶3.53

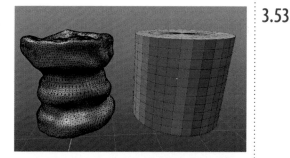

3.53

Next, position the low-poly mesh (whatever it is) over the high-poly mesh, surrounding and containing it. Select the low-poly mesh, and enter *Edit* mode. From *Edit* mode, activate surface snapping, by setting the *Snap* mode to *Face*. The *Snap Target* should be set to *Closest*, to snap vertices to the nearest face in the target mesh. ▶3.54

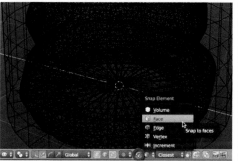

3.54

3 Modeling

3.55

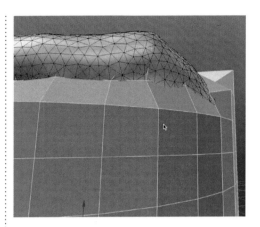

Now you just need to move the vertices in the low-poly mesh, with *Snapping Activated*, to snap them to the nearest point on the destination mesh. By repeating this approach for all vertices, you can snap a low-poly mesh to any high-poly mesh. ▶3.55

3.11 Grease Pencil Modeling

Did you know that you can model, retopologize, and generate geometry using the Grease Pencil? It's amazing stuff! The Grease Pencil is typically regarded as a helper tool for reference purposes. It draws brush strokes inside the viewport, acting as a guide to other artists or as a visual aid for animation. The Grease Pencil doesn't normally show up in renders or animations; it just appears in the viewport as a diagnostic tool. You can draw brush strokes by simply activating the Grease Pencil from the Tool Box (click the *Draw* button), and then start

3.56

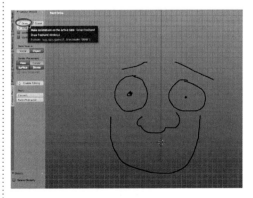

drawing in the viewport by clicking the mouse or pressing on the pen tablet. ▶3.56

Impressively, you can have Blender generate geometry (faces) between brush stroke lines, as though brush strokes defined edge loops within a model. To achieve this, you'll need to activate the *BSurfaces* add-on. Select *File > User Preferences* from the application menu.

Then switch to the *Add-ons* tab. Search for *BSurfaces*, and then enable the add-on. After this, exit the *User Preferences* dialog, saving the changes. ▶3.57

3.57

With the *BSurfaces* add-on enabled, you can easily and quickly retopologize a high-resolution model using the Grease Pencil. To do this, start with a high-resolution model, and then create a plane object from the Tools panel. Select all vertices in the plane object using *Edit* mode, and delete them. Don't delete the object itself, just its vertices. ▶3.58

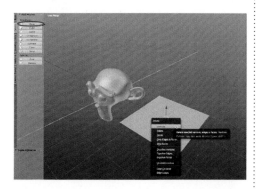

3.58

Next, enter *Edit* mode on the plane object, and switch to the Tools panel, opening the *Grease Pencil* tab. From here, choose *Object* as the *Data Source*, and *Surface* for the *Stroke Placement* field. ▶3.59

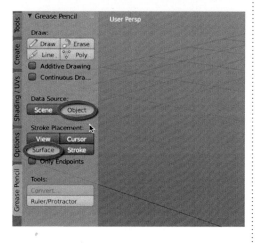

3.59

3 Modeling

3.60

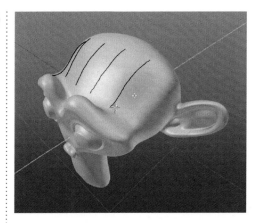

Now, remaining in *Edit* mode for the plane object, use the Grease Pencil draw tool to draw onto the hi-res model. Start drawing lines across the model surface where edge loops should be constructed for a retopologized model. ▶3.60

3.61

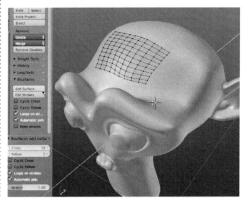

When the lines are drawn, switch to the *Tools* tab of the Tools panel, and expanding the *BSurfaces*, roll out to access the add-on options. From here, click the *Add Surface* button. This generates geometry between the brush strokes, using the strokes as references for inserting edge loops and defining the geometry flow. ▶3.61

3.62

You can control the polygon density using the Tools panel. The fields *Cross* and *Follow* define the horizontal and vertical tessellation of the faces, respectively. ▶3.62

4

UV Mapping Cheats

UV mapping or "unwrapping" is about unraveling a 3D mesh, flattening its faces onto a single plane. This is to assign the mesh a texture map from a 2D texture file, like a PNG or a JPG. UV mapping is the main means used by artists for wrapping a texture around an object, making it look like it is manufactured from real-world materials, like brick or concrete. Blender comes with many powerful options for texture mapping, just like many 3D applications. The main "problem" faced with unwrapping is time. That is, quality UV mapping takes a long time to create—especially for complex, organic models like character heads, trees, and foliage. In this chapter, we'll explore not only some interesting unwrapping methods but also some shortcuts and great time-savers that'll help you be more productive.

4.1

4.1 The UV Image Editor

To access and view an object's UV information, you must use the UV Image Editor. You can access this in different ways. One way is to activate the UV Image Editor interface preset that ships with Blender. Simply choose the *UV Editing* option from the *Interface Pre-set* drop-down menu. The UV image will display as a separate panel on the right-hand side. ▶4.1

4.2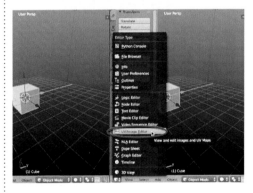

An alternative method is to convert any existing panel or view into the UV Image Editor. Simply click the *Panel* mode icon, and then choose *UV/Image Editor* from the drop-down menu. ▶4.2

4.3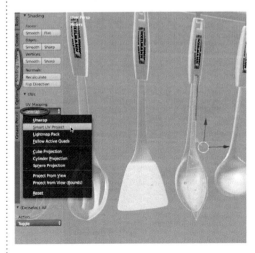

4.2 Smart UV Project

Perhaps the fastest and easiest method of unwrapping a 3D object is Smart UV Project. In most cases, this is a one-button click operation. You simply enter *Edit* mode for the selected object, select all faces, then switch to the *Shading/UVs* tab on the Tools panel, and click *the Unwrap > Smart UV Project* option from the *UV Mapping* drop-down menu. ▶4.3

After this option is selected, Blender displays the Smart UV Project dialog. From here, you can configure how the project will occur. In many cases, the default options work fine. However, for better results, some options may need tweaking. Specifically, try increasing the island margin to add some spacing between separate UV islands, preventing pixels from bleeding across one island to another. In addition, enable the *Correct* and *Stretch* check boxes to maximize the use of texture space. ▶4.4

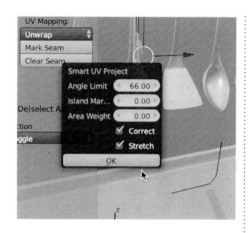

4.4

Smart UV Project is especially effective for hard-surface objects with sharper angles, such as houses, crates, televisions, and tables. But it's less effective for organic and rounded surfaces, such as characters, flowers, mushrooms, trees, cushions, and others. These are often broken into too many different UV islands or clustered together into too large an island. Instead, to map these optimally, run the Smart UV Project as an initial step, and then afterward tweak the mapping manually (see the next section).

4.3 Manual Mapping

The most flexible but time-consuming mapping method is a manual unwrap. This should be used when you're working on a complex object with intricate mapping—lots of rounded surfaces and overlapping UVs. To use this, you must manually mark all seams or cuts in the mesh at edges where

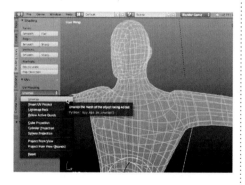

4.5

the mapping should unfold. That is, you should explicitly label each edge where the mesh may be cut apart to be unfolded onto a UV layout. A great way to get started is to run an initial unwrap on your object with the *Unwrap* command. The initial mapping may look very wrong! ▶4.5

4.6

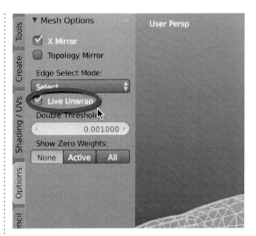

Next, enable the *Live Unwrap* feature from the *Options* tab of the Tools panel, and view your 3D mesh and its mapping side by side in the Blender interface. When *Live Unwrap* is enabled, you can preview the object mapping in real time. This feature continually unwraps your object as you make changes to the edges and seams in the mesh. ▶**4.6**

NOTE

Take care! There are two different *Live Unwrap* options in Blender. One is available from the Tools panel under the *Options* tab, and the other is available via the UVs menu in the UV Image Editor window. These options, unfortunately, don't behave in the same way despite sharing the same name. In this chapter, *Live Unwrap* refers to the feature available from the *Options* tab of the Tools panel, in the 3D view.

Then, from the 3D view, select all edges in the mesh where cuts can be made to split the mapping apart. Then click the *Mark Seam* button from the *Shading/UVs* tab of the Tools panel to affect all the selected edges. When you do this, the selected edges are immediately converted to seams and are marked in red inside the 3D view. This does not change

4.7

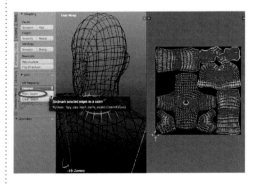

the object topology or structure. In addition, with *Live Unwrap* enabled, the object mapping changes automatically inside the UV Image Editor, as Blender can now unwrap and unfold more of the object. By adding more seams and strategically positioning those seams, you can arrive at a more intuitive map. ▶**4.7**

4.4 Diagnosing and Fixing Map Distortions

Every unwrap operation (whether manual or automatic) involves a conversion between coordinate spaces, as a 3D object is flattened into a 2D space. By flattening a mesh, there's always the risk that its UVs may get distorted, as an artist balances fidelity and quality against an optimal and easy to use UV layout. The aim, in most cases, is not to eliminate *all* distortions but to

minimize distortion so far as is practically possible while also building a sensible and workable UV layout. The Blender UV Image Editor offers some tools for assessing and fixing the extent of distortion, as well as the workability of a specific UV arrangement. Let's see these. ▶**4.8**

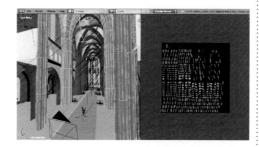

4.8

4.4.1 Stretching and Relaxing

Sometimes UV islands get stretched disproportionally in one or both axes. When this happens, the UV islands no longer match their corresponding area on the mesh in terms of shape—for example, when a cube mesh has UVs that are no longer square. This pulls and twists the texture pixels on the mesh surface, creating distortion. This is usually a bad thing! ▶**4.9**

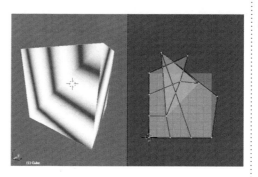

4.9

You can diagnose the amount of stretch on a UV island by using the *Stretch* visualization tool, available from the UV Image Editor N Panel. To do this, expand the N Panel, and enable the *Stretch* check box in the *Display* section. After enabling this, the UV islands become color coded inside the editor. Blue shading defines areas with little or no significant stretching—meaning the UV island shape matches the mesh in that region. In contrast, green areas indicate

4 UV Mapping Cheats

4.10

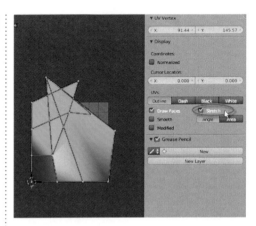

problems—significant stretching between the UVs and the mesh. In green areas, pixels will look distorted on the mesh. ▶4.10

4.11

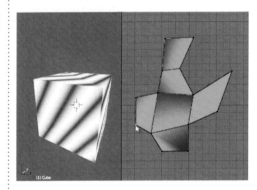

To fix the distortions manually, you should move vertices and faces within the UV Image Editor to change the color coding. This should always be done side by side with the 3D view, to preview the texture mapping on the model as you change the UVs. ▶4.11

4.12

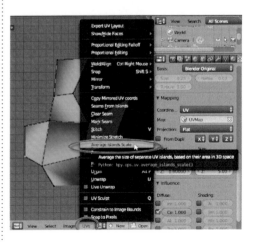

You can fix distortions automatically using the *Minimize Stretch* option. This is accessed by choosing *UVs > Minimize Stretch* from the UV Image Editor menu. When activated, you can roll the middle mouse wheel up and down to contract and expand the UVs for the selected island, interactively reducing its distortion. This option is especially useful for quickly fixing marginally distorted UVs on organic objects like faces, trees, and mushrooms. ▶4.12

More extreme and complex distortions can be fixed using the *Relax* brush of the UV sculpting tool. To access this, start by choosing *UVs > UV Sculpt* from the UV Image Editor window. ▶4.13

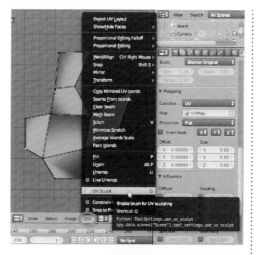

4.13

With *UV Sculpt* enabled, access the Tools panel for the UV Image Editor to customize the brush settings. The *UV Sculpt* tool works like a painter's brush. You can click and drag your mouse or use a pen tablet to interactively paint and move UVs within an island. Access the *Relax* brush by choosing the *Relax* option from the *UV Sculpt* drop-down. In addition, ensure that *Brush Strength* is set to a nonzero value. ▶4.14

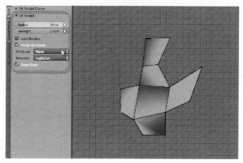

4.14

Then paint onto the UV vertices within the UV Image Editor to reduce stretching. This tool works best when combined with *Stretch Visualization* enabled and by using a weaker brush strength. This lets you immediately see the UV distortion change as you paint and prevents your brush strokes from "overcorrecting." ▶4.15

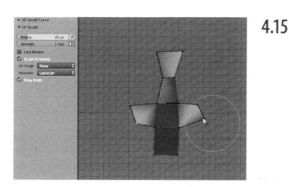

4.15

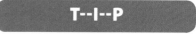

T--I--P

Use the *Relax* brush to perform the bulk of the correction work, and then add finer tweaks manually by moving the vertices individually.

4 UV Mapping Cheats

4.4.2 Checker Patterns

Visualizing Texel distortion is important for creating a solid unwrap and UV layout. Hence, the *Stretch Visualization* tool is highly useful. But distortion is not the only property you'll need to visualize. You'll want to see how UVs are aligned in the layout, to make texture painting easier. And you'll also want to see whether UVs are aligned horizontally or vertically and whether they're flipped or inverted—after all, you don't want textures appearing backward! You can visualize this and more with the UV Grid map. To get started, generate a new UV Grid inside the UV Image Editor—just click the *New* button from the toolbar. ▶4.16

4.16

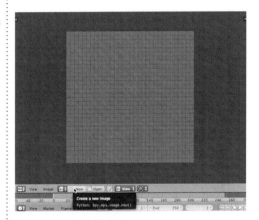

The texture creation dialog appears. Enter a unique texture name, disable the *Alpha* channel, and be sure to choose *Color Grid* from the *Generated Type* drop-down. ▶4.17

4.17

The UV Image Editor fills with a checker-patterned color grid, and alphanumeric references are displayed from bottom to top, left to right. ▶4.18

4.18

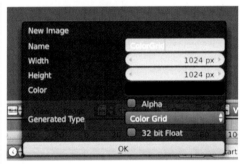

How to Cheat in Blender 2.7x

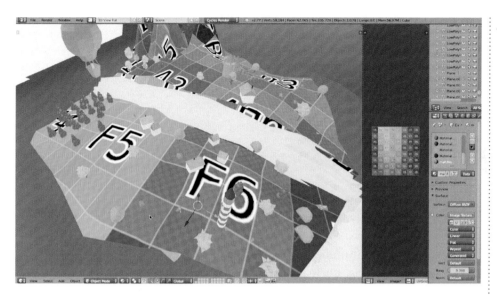

4.19

The UV Grid can then be assigned to a mesh, like a regular texture, and previewed in the viewport to visualize its UV mapping. ▶4.19

So what can the UV Color Grid tell you about an object's mapping, and how? See below.

- *Look for squares:* Study the checker pattern across the object's surface. Do the squares look like squares? Or are they elongated rectangles or curved shapes? If they look like squares (i.e., equal in width and height), then the UVs are not distorted. And that's normally a good thing! If they don't look like squares, then consider revising your UV layout.

- *Look for colors and letters:* The color of a square and its nearby alphanumeric reference tell you about the orientation and arrangement of a UV layout in relation to the mesh. If the letters appear backward or upside down, then your UV layout could be flipped or inverted, respectively, causing your textures to look incorrect. You can fix inverted UVs using the *UVs > Mirror* command, available from the UVs menu inside the UV Image Editor.

- *Compare square size:* Compare the size of squares in the checker pattern across the mesh and across multiple meshes. Generally, squares should be the same size throughout a mesh. When they are, this tells you that the pixels within the texture are being proportionally distributed across the mesh: Larger areas need more pixels. If the squares vary in size, however, then some parts of the mesh may look blurry and low quality by comparison. To correct size issues, you can scale specific UV islands or use the *UVs > Average Islands Scale* command, from the UVs menu in the UV Image Editor. This command rescales all islands, as needed, to reach an average size.

4.5 Camera Mapping

If you need to quickly build a 3D scene from a photograph or an illustration, and if the scene camera doesn't rotate far from its initial orientation during animation, then *camera mapping* is your friend! Camera mapping is great for making animated mountain ranges, city skylines, forests, swamps, corridors and tunnels, nuclear bunkers, dark dungeons, and anything else you can capture with your camera.

4.20

For example, consider making the scene illustrated in 4.20. Here, the camera just gently throbs backward and forward over time to create a menacing ambience. ▶4.20

Without camera mapping, you'd probably model every object using the sculpting tools and polygonal modeling techniques, and then you'd unwrap them either manually or with Smart UV Project. But with camera mapping, you just need to build a rough, proxy model, and then Blender unwraps the model to conform to the initial photograph. This is easy to do and achieves impressive results fast! ▶4.21

4.21

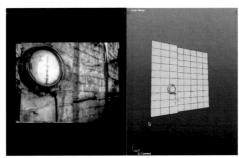

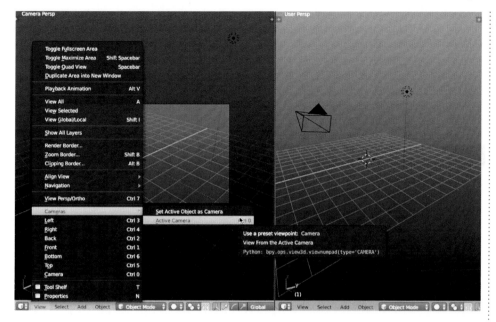

To get started with camera mapping, create a camera object in the scene—if you don't already have one. Then, change your 3D view to the camera perspective. It's important to view your scene from the camera. ▶4.22

Next, use the N Panel to add your photograph as a background to the camera. This lets you see the reference image in the camera viewport and is used to build simple proxy geometry. ▶4.23

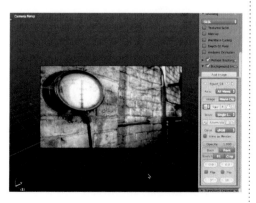

4.23

4.24

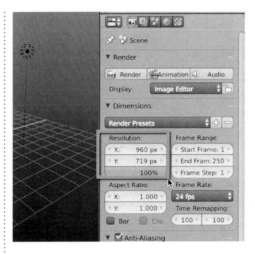

If your background image looks distorted (either too wide or too tall), then change your *Render* dimensions. To do this, switch to the *Render* tab of the Properties panel, and enter the photograph dimensions into the *Resolution X* and *Y* fields. ▶**4.24**

Now comes the tricky part, in two steps! First, use geometric primitives (e.g., cubes and spheres) to block out the basic shapes that define the scene. Use *Edit* mode to refine and tweak the shape. When you've got the basic shapes right, add in extra edge loops, evenly spaced across the geometry (otherwise camera mapping will fail later). To do this, just use the *Loop Cut and Slide* tool. ▶**4.25**

4.25

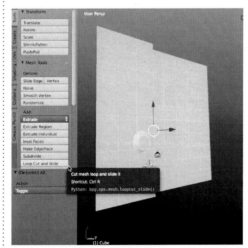

Now view your scene from the camera perspective in the viewport, and try replicating the position, orientation, and focal length of the camera that took the photograph. This ensures your geometry is viewed from the *same angle* as the photograph. This is critical! Use the reference image as a guide: If the photo and your geometry match, then you've got it right! This step requires lots of tweaking and trial and error. It doesn't have to be exact but should be close enough to be believable. ▶**4.26**

4.26

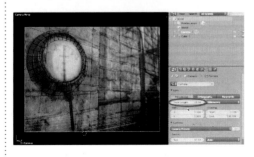

When your camera is configured such that your reference and geometry match up, you can start camera mapping. Start by combining all objects together. Then, in *Edit* mode, select all faces. From the Tools panel, access the *Shading/UVs* tab, and from the *UV Mapping* drop-down, choose the *Project From View* option. ▶4.27

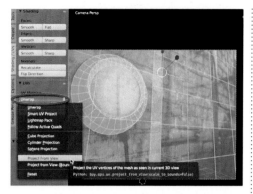

4.27

Open the UV Image Editor, and view your reference photo on top of the newly generated UVs. Everything should match. Some vertices and faces may extend beyond the UV boundaries, but that's fine when camera mapping! ▶4.28

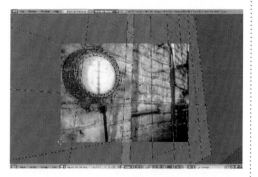

4.28

Now assign the texture to the scene mesh as a *Shadeless* material, and preview the result in the camera viewport, using the *Material* shading mode. The scene should now match the photo. ▶4.29

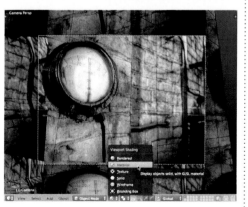

4.29

4.30

If you find the distorted UVs outside the camera border distracting in the viewport, you can hide them. Simply select the camera, and from the *Camera* tab of the Properties panel, enable the option *Passepartout*, and set the *Alpha* field to *1*. This turns the camera border to bold black. ▶4.30

And that's it! Camera mapping is now up and running. You can use this technique to build many complex-looking scenes. Just remember that the effect can be easily broken if your camera rotates too far from its original orientation or moves too far from its starting position.

4.6 Atlas Texturing

A texture atlas is a single image containing many textures. It is a *single* UV space to which *multiple* 3D objects are unwrapped and packed. Mapping objects to a single texture has many practical benefits, especially when making models for games. It's optimal for rendering performance, and it makes texturing simpler as artists work with fewer images. ▶4.31

4.31

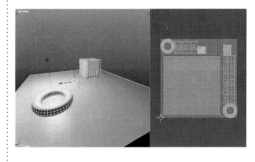

But texture atlases can be practically inconvenient for us as artists. After all, we typically model, unwrap, and texture objects as a separate and unique process—whether we're making a house or a character or a prop. Each object is self-contained and gets its own UV space, which maps to a single, dedicated texture for that object alone. We don't always know in advance how many objects we'll build or whether they should all share the same texture space. And sometimes we'll get completed models from different

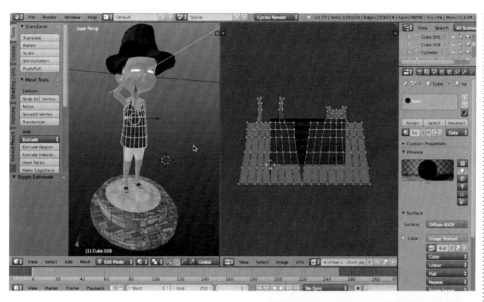

4.32

artists or third parties, which are not laid out in an atlas texture at all. ►4.32

In these cases, and many others, we don't want to invalidate the unwrapping or texture work that has been achieved already if we eventually decide that the object should map into an atlas texture. Thankfully, Blender offers the *Texture Atlas* add-on, which lets us easily map many objects to an atlas and keeps intact any existing mapping. Let's see how. To enable the *Texture Atlas* add-on, open the *User Preferences* window by choosing *File > User Preferences* from the application menu. ►4.33

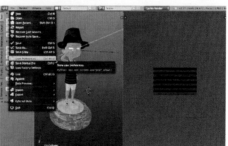

4.33

4.34

From the *User Preferences* dialog, switch to the *Add-ons* tab, and search for *Texture Atlas*. Enable the option *UV: Texture Atlas*, and then press *Save User Settings* to confirm the changes. ►4.34

4.35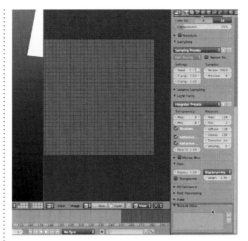

To use the *Texture Atlas* add-on for unwrapping multiple objects, switch to the *Render* tab from the Properties panel. At the bottom of the *Render* tab, there will be a *Texture Atlas* rollout. Expand the tab to reveal the atlas options. ▶4.35

4.36

The *Texture Atlas* rollout maintains a list of all texture atlases in the scene. Each atlas is one texture space to which many different objects can map. To create a new texture atlas, click the + button, and assign the atlas a unique and meaningful name. ▶4.36

4.37

After the atlas is generated, you can adjust the pixel dimensions using the *X* and *Y* dimension drop-down fields. For best performance, especially for game textures, 1:1 aspect ratios are recommended (e.g., square sizes 512 × 512, 1024 × 1024, etc.). ▶4.37

NOTE

Remember, *texture atlas* refers not to a texture image file (like a PNG or JPG) but to a single, consolidated UV space to which many objects may map. Thus, potentially many different texture files could be associated with the UV space.

Next, having created a texture atlas space, we'll need to add objects to it. That is, we'll need to specify which objects in the scene should be unwrapped and included in the texture atlas. This does not invalidate any object's existing mapping. Blender generates an additional UV channel for the object, which is used to contain a new and separate collection of UVs for the atlas. To add objects, select them in the scene, and click the *Add Selected* button from the *Texture Atlas* rollout. ▶4.38

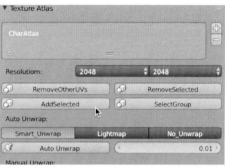

4.38

By default, no visible changes appear to happen. However, by clicking the *StartManualUnwrap* button from the *Texture Atlas* rollout, and then by entering *Edit* mode, you can manipulate the object as though it were a single, combined collection with a unified UV space. With *ManualUnwrap* mode activated, you can safely move, rotate, and scale all UVs into the same UV space without overwriting or destroying the original UVs. ▶4.39

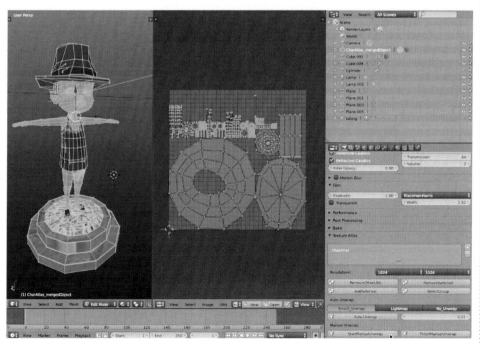

4.39

When you've finished laying out UVs, be sure to click the *FinishManualUnwrap* button from the *Texture Atlas* rollout. This completes the texture atlas unwrapping and restores the objects back to their original states. You can always return to *ManualUnwrap* mode to edit the UVs or add more objects if needed. On leaving *ManualUnwrap* mode, your object's texture may appear different because the viewport is showing its updated atlas UVs as opposed to its original UVs. ▶4.40

4.40

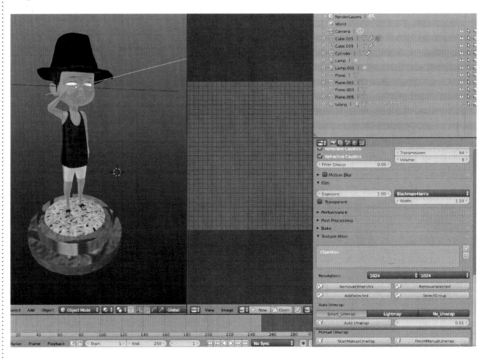

4.41

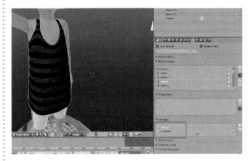

You can easily change any object's UVs between the atlas version and the original from the *Object Data* tab. Simply click the appropriate UV channel from the *UV Maps* list. And voila! ▶4.41

4.7 Packing and Layout

Here's a quick tip. Imagine you've got lots of objects to map onto a single texture atlas, and maybe some objects are composed from many parts. Now this often results in many different UV islands inside the UV Image Editor. When unwrapping, you *could* pack these islands manually into the UV space, one by one, by moving, rotating, and scaling them in place. But there's an easier and semi-automated alternative that can make your life easier. Simply select all UVs, with the mesh in *Edit* mode, and then choose *UVs > Pack Islands* from the UV Image Editor window. When you do this, all islands will automatically position and adjust to fit and fill the available UV space. ▶4.42

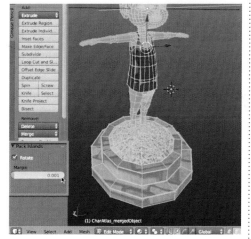

4.42

4.43

Even after the command has been run, you can tweak and edit how it works from the Tools panel inside the 3D view. The *Rotate* check box indicates whether Blender may auto-rotate the islands to produce a better fit, and the *Margin* field allows you to insert a margin of pixels between the islands. ▶4.43

4.8 Copying UVs

So you've spent a long time creating a UV layout for a complex object (e.g., a character), and then you realize that your scene is filled with many copies of the object, and these are not unwrapped. The intention in this case, then, is to transfer the mapping from one object to the duplicates, to save you from unwrapping each object separately or from deleting and reduplicating all the objects. To copy the UVs

4.44

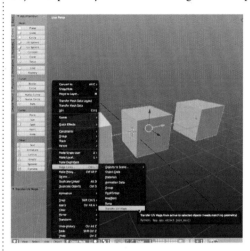

from one object to another, first select the non-unwrapped objects (objects without mapping), and then select the unwrapped object. Then, from the 3D menu, choose *Object > Make Links > Transfer UV Maps.* ▶**4.44**

Afterward, all the selected objects will share the same UV mapping. This procedure only works where objects share the same topology—that is, an identical arrangement of vertices, edges, and faces.

4.9 Overlapping UVs

Overlapping UVs are simply UV islands that intersect (overlap with) each other within the same UV space. This essentially means that two or more different faces in

4.45

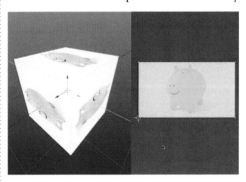

a mesh are mapped to the same texture space. This comes with benefits and disadvantages, and these are worth considering. ▶**4.45**

- *Do* overlap UVs when multiple faces always look the same and you want to maximize texture space.

- *Do* overlap UVs when many faces look identical and you later intend baking out an object's textures to a second set of nonoverlapped UVs.
- *Don't* overlap UVs when baking light maps.
- *Don't* overlap UVs when exporting models to game engines, unless the engine will never bake or render to the textures.

4.10 Breaking Islands

When you unwrap an object, it'll normally be broken down into separate UV islands or shells. These are self-contained areas of faces. ▶4.46

4.46

You can easily stitch multiple islands together to form even larger islands, but it's not clear how to break them apart inside the UV Editor. Here's how. First, activate the option *Keep UV and Edit Mode in Synch*, using the UV Editor toolbar. ▶4.47

4.47

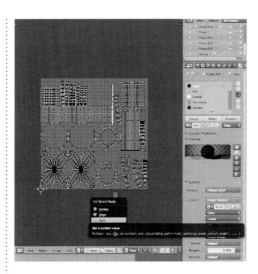

4.48

When you activate this option, you can select faces and vertices in the mesh independently of UVs in the UV Image Editor. Thus, by switching to *Face* selection mode in the UV Image Editor, you can now select and move faces around, pulling them apart from their island. This approach works great for breaking apart existing islands into new, smaller islands. ▶4.48

4.11 Exporting UV Layouts

After creating a UV layout, you'll probably want to perform some texture-painting work inside Photoshop or GIMP to make your textures look great. In preparation for this, it's a good idea to export an image file outlining your complete UV layout—the lines, edges, shapes, and perimeters. This gives you a good idea, as a reference, about where your UV islands are within the texture space, so you can paint details exactly where they need to be. You can achieve this by exporting the UV layout to an image file with a transparent background. To do this from the UV Image Editor, select all UVs, and then choose *UVs > Export UV Layout* from the UV Image Editor menu. ▶4.49

4.49

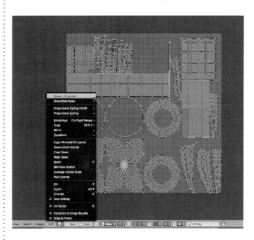

4.12 The 0–1 Space

Most UV spaces are square, equal in width and height. Typically, this is called the 0–1 space, and all your UVs should fit inside this region. You can easily ensure that UVs don't overextend this region by choosing *UVs > Constrain to Image Bounds*. Using this option, you can't move any UV islands outside the 0–1 space. Great stuff! ▶4.50

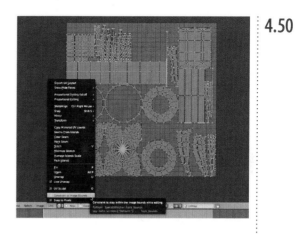

4.50

4.13 Pinning and Unwrapping

If you select all faces in a mesh and choose from any of the unwrapping options, like Smart UV Project, Blender automatically unwraps all selected faces. This is useful for quickly unwrapping an object. ▶4.51

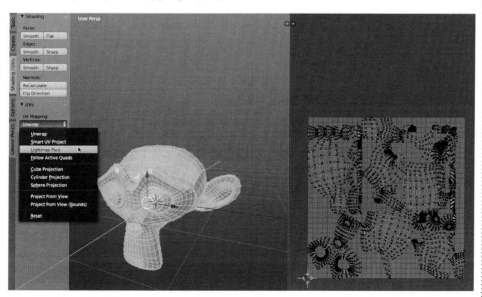

4.51

The problem is that *all* faces influence the unwrap. This means that if you've previously spent time unwrapping a part of the mesh manually, then all those changes will be overwritten by the automatic methods. You can prevent this happening by using *pinning.* The *Pin* method lets you choose vertices to hold in position, and these will remain in place and be unaffected by any automatic mapping methods. Simply select all vertices to hold in place, and then choose *UVs > Pin* from the UV Image Editor menu, or else press the *P* keyboard shortcut. ▶4.52

4.52

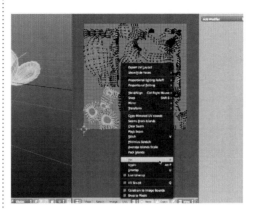

5
Texturing and Materials

Textures and materials are critical for making objects look realistic and stylized. A texture refers to a collection of pixels, either from an image file (like a PNG) or procedurally generated by an algorithm that specifies how a mesh surface should appear. A material specifies how one or more textures work together, in combination with scene lighting, to produce the final shading of a model when viewed from the render camera. Without textures and materials, objects would have no shading. Blender offers many tools for building believable materials and textures. This chapter considers not just these tools specifically but also clever ways of working with them to get the diffuse texture you need, faster and more easily than you might expect. Let's take a look.

5 Texturing and Materials

5.1 Blender Render versus Cycles

Blender supports multiple render systems, most notably Blender Internal and Cycles. A popular view is that these are mutually exclusive systems (you can't use both) and each is responsible for rendering your objects and scenes. Following

from this, these people agree that Cycles is a more feature-filled and powerful system. Now, in many respects this is true. ▶5.1

However, if you view these two systems as complementary rather than competitive, you can achieve interesting results. Some features are supported better in Blender Internal and some better in Cycles. And it's important to recognize this to get the most from Blender. Later sections will specify where a specific render system should be preferred.

5.2 Viewport Rendering

Both Blender Internal and Cycles support *viewport rendering*. This lets you continuously preview renders from within a viewport, giving you real-time feedback about the look of your scene. Using viewport rendering, you get to see how your

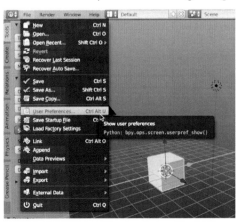

textures and materials look under scene lighting, complete with glossiness, bump, and displacement. Depending on your hardware, run-time performance differs dramatically, and on some Mac computers it may even freeze the software (unfortunately)! To activate viewport rendering, start by enabling hardware acceleration from the *User Preferences* dialog. To do this, select *File > User Preferences*. ▶5.2

Switch to the *System* tab, and from here change the *Compute Device* from *None* to *CUDA* (for Windows) or *OpenCL* (for Mac). In the drop-down menu below, select the graphics device to be used for rendering. By doing this, you delegate the rendering workload to your graphics hardware, as opposed to the CPU. This improves render performance, including viewport rendering. ▶5.3

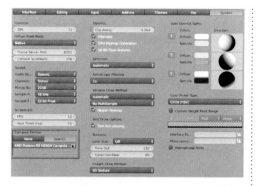

5.3

Next, activate viewport rendering by changing the *Viewport Shading* mode to *Rendered*. This is accessed via the 3D view menu. ▶5.4

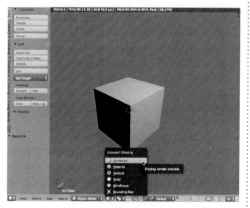

5.4

Viewport rendering is computationally expensive. It easily causes major system slowdowns. A simple way to mitigate this is to use viewport rendering only for *a smaller, secondary 3D viewport*—as opposed to the main 3D viewport. ▶5.5

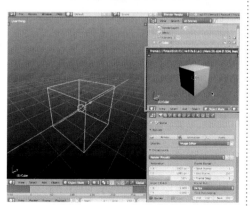

5.5

5 Texturing and Materials

5.3 Layered Painting: Blender Internal

Texture painting lets you paint weighted brushstrokes and images onto 3D models directly in the viewport, using either the mouse or the pen tablet. It makes texture creation simple and more intuitive and is especially useful for hiding texture seams. Not only this, but you can paint on layers too, just like painting with Photoshop or GIMP—stacking up brushstrokes on top of each other! This means you have

5.6

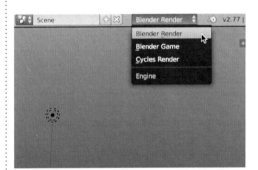

access to a largely nondestructive texture painting workflow directly in the Blender interface. By painting onto separate layers, you can carefully organize and isolate specific brushstrokes and pixels. Texture painting, however, is more feature filled with the Blender Internal engine, as opposed to Cycles. Consequently, before texture painting objects, activate the Blender Internal renderer from the application toolbar. ▶5.6

5.7

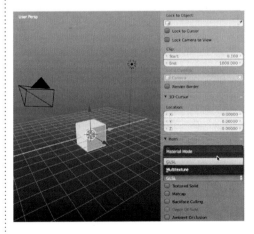

To get started with layered texture painting, display the N Panel inside the 3D view. From the *Shading* section, select *GLSL* from the *Shading* drop-down. Using *GLSL* mode, you can preview texture painting work using the *Texture* and *Material* viewport shading modes. The default *Multitexture* mode will not display texture paint edits. ▶5.7

Select a mesh to texture paint, assign it some UV mapping, remove its materials, and then enter *Texture Paint* mode by choosing *Texture Paint* from the mode drop-down. ▶5.8

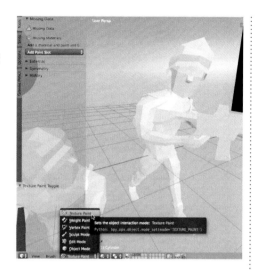

5.8

By opening the Tools panel, you can access the texture-painting tools and their associated settings. Select the *Tools* tab, and a "Missing Data" warning appears. This warning indicates that no paint layers (slots) exist and the object has no material assigned. You can fix this in one operation by creating a new paint slot—and Blender does the rest! To achieve, this click the *Add Paint Slot* drop-down button from the *Tools* tab. Then choose the kind of slot to add. The slot type specifies the material channel to which your brushstrokes are applied— such as *Diffuse*, *Bump*, *Glossiness*, and so on. In many cases, the initial slot will be *Diffuse Color*, allowing you to paint color data into the main material channel. ▶5.9

5.9

The *Add Texture Paint Slot* dialog appears. Use this to specify the pixel width and height of a new diffuse texture. Clicking *OK* creates a new texture and assigns it to the *Diffuse* slot for the currently active material. If the object has no material, Blender automatically makes one. If the texture is an initial background (or base) layer, then you don't need to create an *Alpha Channel*. ▶5.10

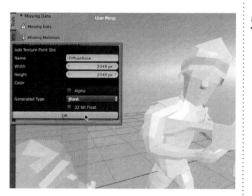

5.10

5 Texturing and Materials

5.11

The *Slots* tab displays a complete list of available paint slots (layers), each of which maps to a texture for painting. The slots correspond to textures assigned to the material for the selected object. These can be viewed from the *Textures* tab in the Properties panel. ▶5.11

5.12

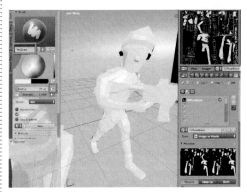

Now select a brush to use for painting (like the *Texture Draw* brush) from the *Tools* tab. All brushstrokes are applied to the selected slot from the *Slots* tab. The *Radius* and *Strength* settings control properties for the brush, and these can be linked directly to the pressure sensitivity of your pen tablet through the *Pressure* button. ▶5.12

5.13

Now here comes the clever layer painting part! Create a new layer by switching to the *Slots* tab and clicking the *Add Texture Paint Slot* drop-down button. From here, choose *Diffuse Color*. Then, select a new diffuse texture. For the new layer, ensure that *Alpha Channel* is activated. ▶5.13

For the *Color* field, select a color with an *Alpha* (*A*) of *0*. This fills the new texture slot and texture with transparent pixels, showing the layer beneath. ▶5.14

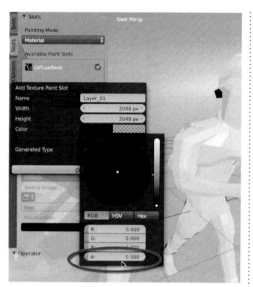

Now select the newly created slot from the *Slots* tab, and continue the painting process as before. This time, all new paint strokes are added to the new slot and are *layered on top* of the original layer. You can easily toggle layer visibility on and off using the visibility icon from the *Slots* tab. And you can also change the *Blend* mode of the selected slot, using the *Blend Type* drop-down. The *Blend* modes work much like Photoshop or GIMP blend modes. ▶5.15

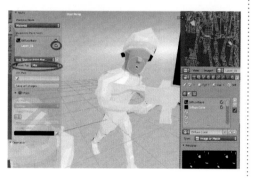

5.15

5.4 Flattening Layer Painting

Imagine this: You've invested time and effort painting layer after layer of brushstrokes, and your model is finally looking great. But now you need to flatten all layers, exporting the consolidated paint to a single, diffuse texture—the kind used for any real-time game engine. How can you do this? Blender doesn't have

5.16

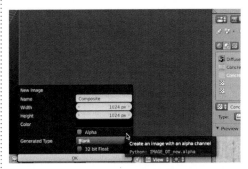

a convenient *Flatten* button. The way to achieve layer flattening is to use *texture baking*. To start, use the UV Image Editor to create a new texture that will contain the flattened output. Select *Image > New Image* from the file menu. Then, create a new texture with the needed dimensions, without an *Alpha Channel*. ▶**5.16**

5.17

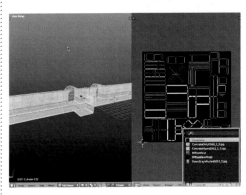

Next, select all the faces in your model using *Edit* mode, and then view your composite, output texture from the UV Editor, side by side with the model. ▶**5.17**

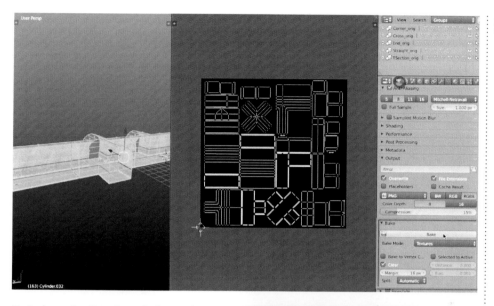

Switch to the *Render* tab from the Properties panel. Scroll down to the *Bake* section. From *Bake* mode, choose *Textures*. Then click the *Bake* button. Voila! ▶5.18

Now you've got a completely baked diffuse texture from your painted layers, and you'll want to export it to an external file. To do this, just choose *Image > Save As Image* from the UV Image Editor. ▶5.19

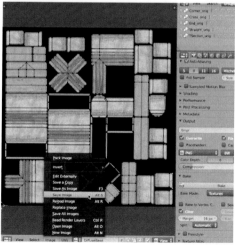

5.5 Camera Project Painting

Here's a great tip. You've created a mesh and unwrapped it (although you've not yet textured it), and now you've positioned the scene camera to get a complementary view of your work under some basic lighting. You're now ready to make an initial render. ▶5.20

5.20

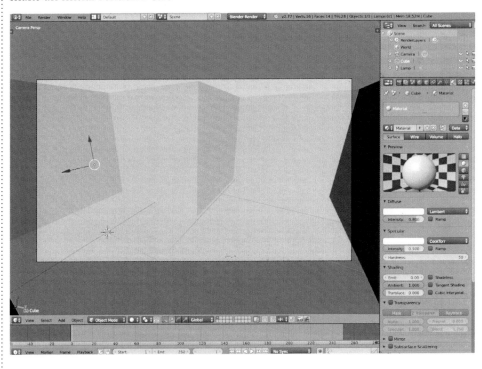

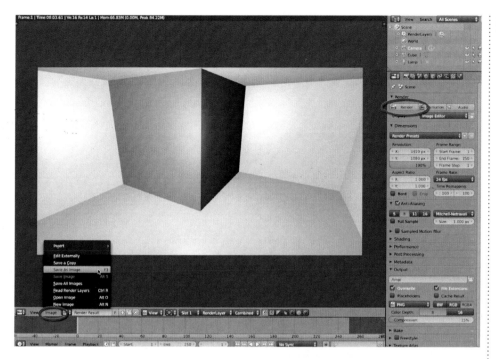

After making a full-size render from the camera using any render engine (Internal or Cycles), save the result to a standard PNG image file, using the UV Image Editor. ▶5.21

At this stage, a texture artist or a Photoshop expert may wish he or she could import the rendered image into

Photoshop, paint all texture details *onto the rendered image* (using it as a guide) with Photoshop's expansive painting tools, and then finally save the result, projecting it back onto the model in Blender as a final texture. Well, you *can* do this! Here's how. First, create a new layer in Photoshop on top of the rendered image. This should contain all paint details to be projected back onto the model. The rendered image acts only as a background reference to guide your painting. ▶5.22

5.23

Now paint your details onto the detail layer. You can use the standard Photoshop brush tools or even the *Vanishing Point* filter to project images into perspective on the render. Repeat this process until you get an image that looks correct for your needs. ▶5.23

5.24

When you're done, hide the rendered background layer to reveal the transparent pixels beneath, and save the result as a transparent PNG file. This allows you to save the details painted without saving the rendered background, which was intended as a reference only. ▶5.24

5.25

Next, load the image into Blender as a texture via the UV Image Editor. Choose *Image > Open Image* from the editor menu, and select the PNG texture from your hard drive. ▶5.25

Now activate *Texture Painting* mode on your 3D model, and switch to the Tools panel. From the Tools panel, expand the *External* rollout, and enter the image dimensions of your saved render. In my case, it was 1920 × 1080. ▶5.26

5.26

5.27

Then click the *Apply Camera Image* button, and choose your imported image. When you do this, the image texture is project painted onto the model, from the active camera, and then saved to the model's texture via its UV mapping. ▶5.27

Great! You've now project painted a texture onto your model. This technique makes it really easy to apply Photoshop paint work onto your geometry. In addition, you can project paint onto a model from multiple camera angles, multiple times, and on selected faces. This gives you even more control over texture-painting models. For the best results, however, project paint from orthographic views, as this minimizes texture distortion from perspective angles.

5

5.6 Flat Projection

If you're rendering a scene for only a single frame at a fixed and known camera angle, then *flat projection* is your friend. It can save you lots of unwrapping time and work. This is especially useful for creating product shots, visualizations, and promotional renders. This technique is similar to, though distinct from, camera mapping. ▶5.28

5.28

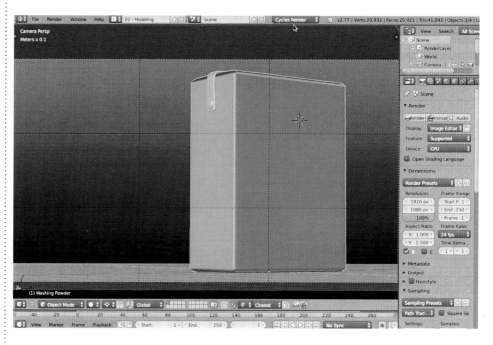

The basic idea is that you only need to unwrap and texture a model in the areas that are definitely going to be seen. If you're not rendering an animation and your model is seen from only one camera angle, then you only need to unwrap and texture for that angle. You can unwrap a model quickly and easily from the viewpoint of the camera, which is known as flat projection. To do this, switch the 3D view to camera view, using the keyboard shortcut *Ctrl + 0*, or use the menu *View > Camera*. ▶5.29

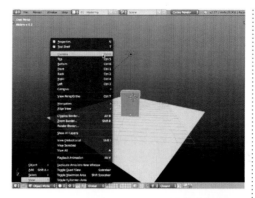

5.29

Next, enter *Edit* mode for your model, and select all faces. Then, open the *Shading/UVs* tab of the Tools panel, and choose *Project From View* from the *UV Mapping* drop-down list. ▶5.30

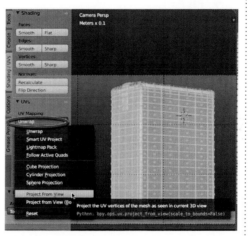

5.30

After this, the model is unwrapped based on the camera view. This lets you easily overlay the UVs onto an existing texture, if you have one, or you can texture paint over the UVs—even directly in the UV Image Editor. This reduces texture-painting work as you only paint the areas that are in view. ▶5.31

5.31

5.32

Once you've aligned the camera-projected UVs to a texture, you can quickly get impressive, photo-realistic results. Good work! ▶5.32

5.7 UV Cloning

Sometimes, after modeling, unwrapping, and then texture painting a model for a project, you'll want to reuse or repurpose that asset for a different project to save time. When doing this, you may need to change the object's UV mapping, either entirely by creating a new set of UVs or by moving the existing ones into a larger UV arrangement, like a texture atlas. In either case, you'll invalidate the texture because the texture will no longer match the new UVs. But, thankfully, there's an easy way to fix this by using *UV cloning*. ▶5.33

5.33

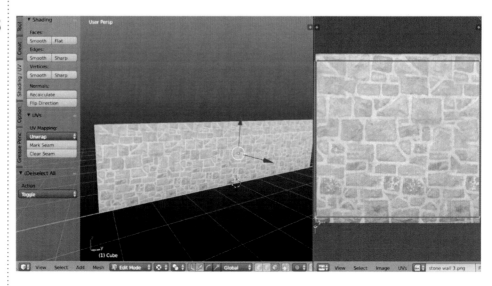

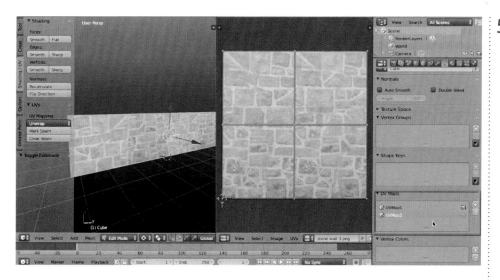

5.34

UV cloning lets you take two different UV sets and two textures and paint from one texture onto the other, transferring the pixels between the UV sets. To get started, make sure your object has two UV channels, the original UVs and the newer, destination UVs. ▶5.34

Next, enter *Texture Paint* mode for the selected object, and create two new paint slots. The first paint slot should be associated with the completed, original texture already mapped to the object through the original UVs. The second slot should be associated with an empty, blank texture, associated with the destination UVs. ▶5.35

5.35

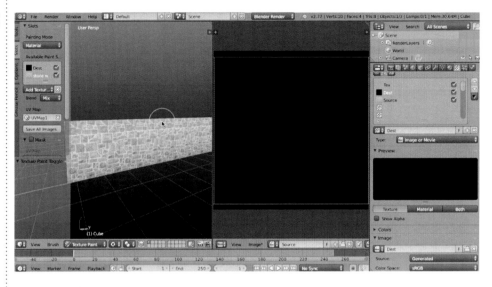

5.36

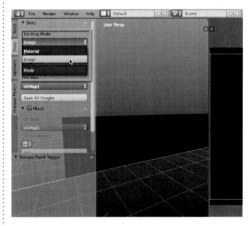

From the *Slots* tab, change the *Painting* mode from *Material* to *Image*. This is because we'll be working with images and texture exclusively, as opposed to whole materials. ▶5.36

Change to the *Tools* tab, and select *Clone Brush* for painting. The *Clone* brush works like the Clone-Stamp tool in Photoshop and GIMP. That is, it samples pixels at a relative location from a texture and then paints those pixels relatively to a destination texture. ▶5.37

5.37

On selecting *Clone Brush*, Blender assumes you'll be cloning pixels within the same texture and same UV space. For this reason, activate the check box *Clone from image/UV map*. This lets us specify a different texture and UV space as the *Clone Source*. ▶5.38

5.38

Then choose the *source* texture (the *original* texture) for the *Source Clone Image* field. And choose its associated UV channel for *the Source Clone UV Map* field. In short, this is the texture and UV space from which you're copying. ▶5.39

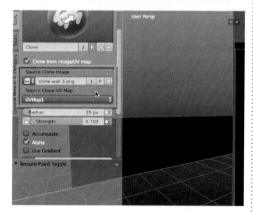

5.39

5.40

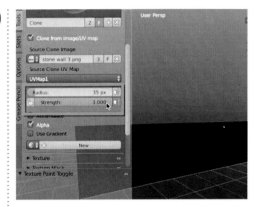

Move the *Brush Strength* to *1.00* (full strength). This prevents the *Clone* brush from diluting the brushstrokes when painted to the destination. ▶**5.40**

Now switch to the *Slots* tab, and choose the destination texture from the *Canvas Image* drop-down, and choose the destination UVs from the *UV Map* drop-down. ▶**5.41**

5.41

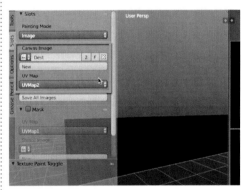

Finally! Now use the *Clone* brush to paint across the model surface in large and expansive brushstrokes, and you'll transfer the texture data from one texture to another across different UVs. Excellent! And you can tweak the brush color and shape to add interesting effects if you want to change the texture slightly. ▶**5.42**

5.42

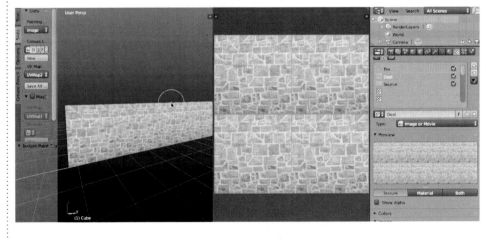

Don't forget! Once you've finished painting your new texture, save it to an external image file from the UV Image Editor. ▶5.43

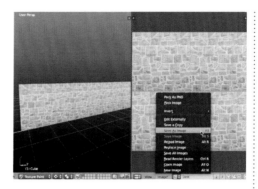

5.43

5.8 Configuring a Stencil Brush

A *Stencil* brush is a standard brush, accessible in *Texture Paint* mode, that projects a texture into the scene for painting onto an intersecting model. It's a great way to quickly paint details from image files. A texture is aligned over the mesh in the viewport, and intersecting brushstrokes paint the texture to the model. ▶5.44

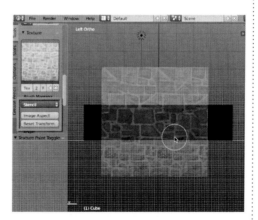

5.44

However, if you're using the Maya control scheme instead of the Blender scheme, then you're in for a problem. By default, the Maya controls leave the *Stencil* brush undefined, without any keyboard or mouse shortcuts, and so you can't practically use it. You can't move, rotate, or resize the *Stencil* brush in the viewport. Thankfully, however, this can be fixed. Let's see how. ▶5.45

5.45

5.46

Open the *User Preferences* window by choosing *File > User Preferences* from the application file menu. Then switch to the *Input* tab. Here, you can customize application controls, both keyboard and mouse. ▶5.46

5.47

Next, expand the *3D View > Image Paint* rollouts in the control hierarchy. This is where the *Stencil* brush control definitions should be. ▶5.47

5.48

Now click the *Add New* button to create a new keyboard/mouse binding. This expands a new control definition panel. ▶5.48

5.49

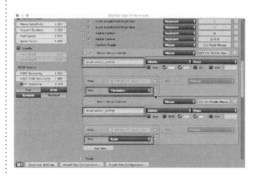

Add two new definitions—one for *Stencil* brush *Translation* and the other for *Stencil* brush *Scale*. The command *brush.stencil_control* must be entered into the command field for each entry, and then an operation must be chosen from the *Tool* field. Initially, the *Tool* field appears grayed out and disabled, but you can activate the option by clicking it. ▶5.49

For *Stencil* brush *Translation*, I've used the keyboard shortcut *Shift + Ctrl + Middle Mouse*. For *Stencil* brush *Scaling*, I've used *Ctrl + Alt + Middle Mouse*. Be sure to save the controls. ▶5.50

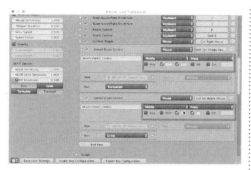

5.50

Now let's test those controls by using the *Stencil* brush. Activate *Texture Paint* mode for the selected object, and pick a standard *Texture Draw* brush from the Tools panel. ▶5.51

5.51

Expand the *Texture* tab rollout for the brush, and click the swatch to choose a loaded image texture for stencil painting. ▶5.52

5.52

5.53

Now activate *Stencil* brush mode from the *Textures* rollout by selecting *Stencil* from the *Brush Mapping* drop-down. ▶5.53

5.54

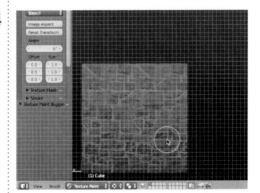

When you do this, a rectangular projection of the texture appears inside the 3D viewport. When your brushstrokes and the texture intersect geometry in the viewport, you can paint texture details onto your model. ▶5.54

5.55

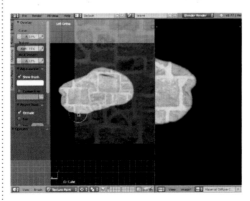

Excellent! You can now move and resize the texture *Stencil* brush using your newly configured controls. ▶5.55

5.9 Node Wrangler

When building Cycles materials, you'll frequently use the Blender Node Editor. This editor lets you make materials by building a node graph. The basic idea and craft is to drag, drop, and connect together functional nodes into a meaningful arrangement. This arrangement defines how a material finally shades the surface of a model. There are many nodes available and many ways of combining and connecting them, giving you practically limitless potential for building materials. ▶5.56

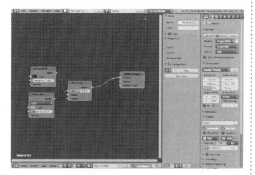

5.56

To increase your speed and productivity with the Node Editor, you can enable the *Node Wrangler* add-on. This add-on offers you miscellaneous shortcuts, menus, and features to enhance your workflow, as we'll see. To enable the add-on, open the *User Preferences* window by choosing *File > User Preferences* from the application menu. Then switch to the *Add-ons* tab, and enable the *Node Wrangler* add-on. ▶5.57

5.57

The Node Wrangler includes many keyboard shortcuts. You can view a complete list of these at any time by expanding the *Node Wrangler* entry in the *Add-ons* tab and clicking *Show Hotkey List*. ▶5.58

5.58

5.59

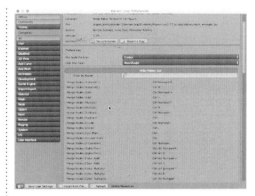

5.60

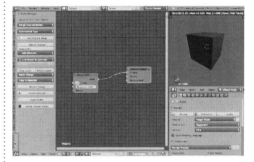

5.61

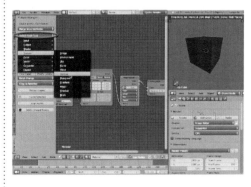

Doing this lists all keyboard shortcuts for the *Node Wrangler,* and these take effect inside the Node Editor. One of the most important is *Ctrl + Space.* ▶**5.59**

When the *Node Wrangler* add-on is enabled, you can access many of its feature from the Tools panel, inside the Node Editor window. From the Tools panel, click the *Node Wrangler* tab. You can also access the same options by pressing *Ctrl + Space* on the keyboard. ▶**5.60**

So what does Node Wrangler do, specifically? Many things. Here are some. First, you can easily change a node type, even after it's been added to the graph. For example, if you add a *Texture* node, connecting it to other graph nodes, and then later decide to change it, you can do that! You don't need to disconnect or reconnect anything. Just select the node, and then choose *Switch Node type* from the Tools menu, choosing a new type for the selected node. ▶**5.61**

You can also create frames or borders around groups of nodes to organize them visually. Doing this does not affect their function or relation to other nodes—only how they appear in the graph. To do this, box select a group of related nodes, and click the *Frame Selected* button from the Tools panel. ▶5.62

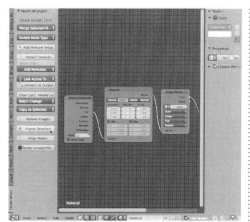

5.62

After creating a border or frame, you can use the N Panel to customize its color. By using your own personal, color-coded system, you can quickly identify node groups by function in the graph. ▶5.63

You can get more information about the Node Wrangler, and its full feature set, online at https:// wiki.blender.org/index.php/ Extensions:2.6/Py/Scripts/Nodes/ Node_Wrangler

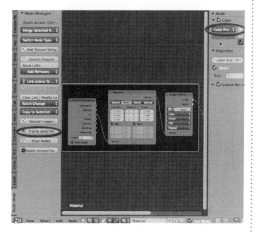

5.63

5.10 Stroke Methods

Blender offers many interesting and lesser known stroke methods during texture painting. These control how a texture-draw brush behaves, and they can be found

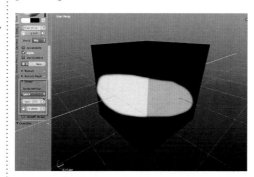

in the *Stroke* rollout, from the Tools menu, while *Texture Paint* mode is active for the selected mesh. The default method is *Space*. This simply lays down equally spaced circles onto the mesh, one atop the other, for as long as the brush is painting, and this creates the effect of a standard brushstroke. ▶5.64

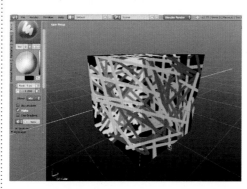

By clicking on the *Stroke Method* drop-down, you can change the stroke method. This is useful when you have very specific painting requirements. If you need to paint lines or to create very long and narrow stripe-style effects, you can use the *Line* method. After activating *Line*, simply click and drag on the mesh to draw a line, based on the brush color, size, and opacity settings. ▶5.65

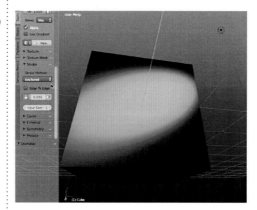

Anchored mode keeps the brush position constant after clicking, and mouse movement changes the radius. This can be especially useful for simulating spotlight effects and shadows. ▶5.66

If you need dots, trails, speckles, stars, droplets, and other noise-based effects, consider the *Airbrush* method. When it is activated, use the *Rate* type-in field to control the time delay (in seconds) between brushstrokes. Lower values create denser and more populated strokes. ▶5.67

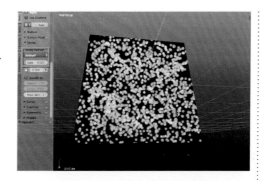

5.67

Maybe you're creating an old-school sci-fi control panel or console for a spaceship, and you need to precisely position lights, glows, and flickering warning signals. You can do this using the *Drag Dot* method. This allows you to create and initially position a single brushstroke dot with a mouse click, and then you can drag and move the same dot around until you're happy with its position. This method is useful when you need to precisely align brushstrokes. ▶5.68

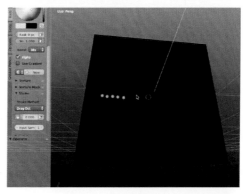

5.68

I've saved the best method for last! Using the *Curve* method, you can lay down a set of points to draw a curve, along with Bezier handles, and then draw the curve onto the mesh. This gives you extensive drawing potential. To use this, first select the *Curve* option for the *Stroke Method*. ▶5.69

5.69

5.70

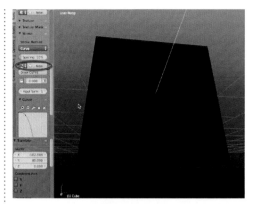

Then click the *New* button from the Tools panel to create a new curve. You can create as many different curves as you need. ▶5.70

5.71

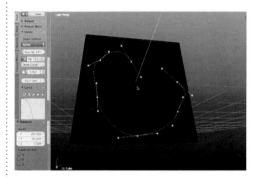

After creating a new curve definition, press *Ctrl + Click* inside the viewport to draw the curve. You can even click and drag the existing handles and points to reshape the curve, as in a vector-drawing application. ▶5.71

5.72

If your keyboard and mouse controls don't work as intended, you can easily customize them via the *User Preferences* window, from the *Input* tab. Search for *Add Curve Point and Slide*. ▶5.72

When you've defined a curve in the viewport, you're ready to paint it onto the mesh as pixel data. To do this, align the model and curve in the viewport, and click the *Draw Curve* button. This uses the *Brush, Strength*, and *Opacity* settings to project paint a curve onto the model, based on the drawn curve. ▶5.73

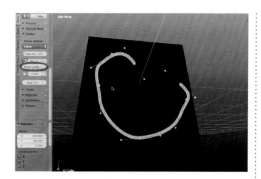

5.73

6

Rigging and Animation Cheats

Animation is about applying meaningful changes to models and scenes over time, and *rigging* is about structuring them to animate more easily. Animation and rigging together cover many tasks, from making bouncing balls and logo cut scenes to rendering camera fly-throughs and walking characters. In addition, there are many types of animation: key frame animation, procedural animation, blend shapes and morphs, armatures, hierarchical animation, and others. In this chapter, we'll explore many tips and tricks for animating and rigging more effectively, in the widest sense possible. Some of these tips save you time, some introduce features you may not have known about, and some just show you new perspectives on familiar features. So let's roll up our sleeves, mix up our metaphors, and jump in.

6.1 Keyframing, Auto-Key, and Optimization

The *key frame* is the raw ingredient of any animation. Key frames mark critical moments where change occurs to one or more objects. By creating

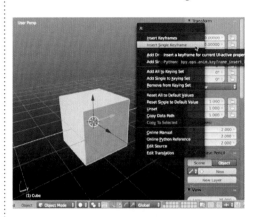

6.1

a key frame for an object *x* at time *t*, you're essentially defining the *state* of *x* at time *t*. When you create multiple key frames, Blender generates animation automatically, by interpolating *between* the key frames, using an *F curve*. You can manually create key frames for most editable fields of an object at any time. For example, to keyframe an object's position, hover your cursor over the *X*, *Y*, or *Z* fields from the N Panel, and right click your mouse, choosing *Insert Single Keyframe*. The field highlights yellow, indicating that a key frame was created. ▶6.1

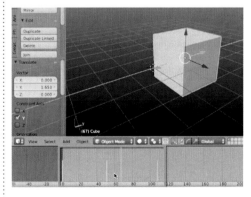

6.2

After creation, key frames appear in the timeline window too, as vertical yellow bars. This indicates their position within an animation. ▶6.2

Creating key frames is an important but tedious process, especially if you have lots to create manually. Thankfully, Blender can auto-generate key frames based on the changes you make to objects. This saves you a lot of work. This feature is called *Auto-Key*, and you can enable it via the *User Preferences* window. To do this, access *User Preferences* by choosing *File > User Preferences* from the application menu. Switch to the *Editing* tab, and select the button *Auto Keyframing*. ▶6.3

Once it is activated, also make sure that *Auto-Key* is activated from the *Animation Timeline* window. To do this, activate the *Auto-Key* button from the bottom toolbar of the Animation Timeline. ▶6.4

Now all editable properties for objects will be keyframed automatically when changed. To confirm this, Blender color codes all keyframed fields, turning them yellow. ▶6.5

6.3

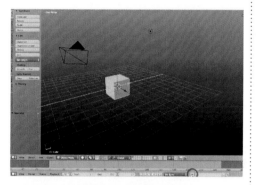

6.4

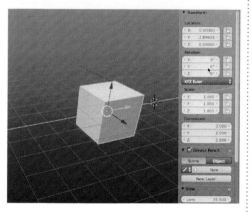

6.5

6.6

6.7

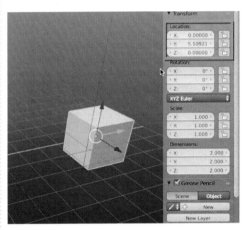

You can improve this workflow even further. On key frame generation, Blender often keyframes more properties than are truly necessary. For position changes, for example, Blender keyframes all position, rotation, and scale fields by default, rather than just position. This leads to an excess. You can cut down on unnecessary key frames with auto-key by enabling the *Only Insert Needed* option. This is available via the *User Preferences* dialog. Switch to the *Editing* tab, and activate the *Only Insert Needed* check box. On activation, Blender *only* keyframes the essential properties, keeping key frames to a minimum. This makes animations clearer and tidier. ▶6.6

Now, on changing objects with auto-key activated, Blender keyframes only needed properties. Great! ▶6.7

6.2 Motion Paths: Following and Clamping

Whether you're animating people, cars, airplane, bicycles, animals, guided missiles, or something else, you'll often need objects to travel a path or a trajectory. You *could*, in theory, keyframe this kind of motion manually and automatically, by simple translating and rotating your object appropriately throughout the animation duration, creating key frames where needed. But in this case, it's often easier to draw a spline object, representing the path, and have our object follow that. In this section, we'll see two ways to do that: *following* and *clamping*. ▶6.8

First, let's create a path for an object to follow. You can do this using the *Path* object. Access the Tools panel, and from the *Create* tab click the *Path* button. ▶6.9

Select the *Path* object in the viewport, and use *Edit* mode to manipulate the path points, repositioning them to define a travel path. ▶6.10

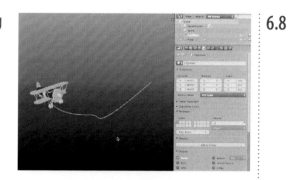

6.8

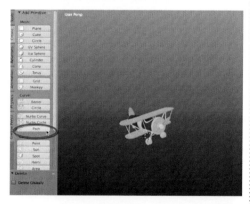

6.9

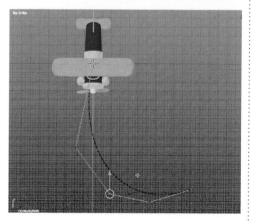

6.10

6.11

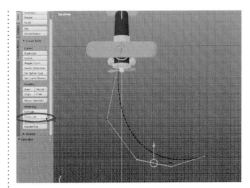

You can add more control points to the curve, if needed, by selecting any two points on the curve and clicking the *Subdivide* button from the Tools menu, from the *Curve Tools* rollout. This inserts an additional control point midway between the two selected control points. ▶6.11

6.12

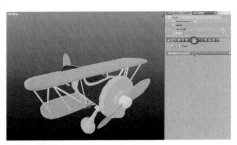

When you have a path and an object that should follow it, you have two options available. Let's see the first one: the *Follow* method. Select your object, and then switch to the *Constraints* tab from the Properties panel. Then choose *Add Object Constraint* to add a new constraint to the object. ▶6.12

6.13

Select *Follow Path* to add a *Follow Path* constraint to the selected object. Then, from the *Target* field, select the path object to follow. Initially, no change occurs in the viewport. ▶6.13

6.14

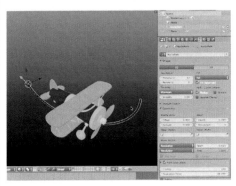

Now select the path object, and switch to the *Spline* tab from the Properties panel. The *Evaluation* field controls the movement of the object along the path. When *Evaluation Time* is *0*, the object is positioned at the start of the path, and when *Evaluation Time* is at *100*, the object is positioned at the end of the path. The values between represent intervening positions. The *Evaluation Time* field can be keyframed to animate the object along the path. ▶6.14

By default, the object doesn't rotate to align its nose with the path as it moves. To achieve this, select your object, and from the *Follow Path* constraint, enable the option *Follow Curve.* ▶6.15

When you do this, the object may immediately rotate to face in the wrong direction. You can easily fix this by using the *Forward* field. Simply choose the local axis that acts as the forward vector. ▶6.16

NOTE

This only works if your object is modeled and aligned to a cardinal axis. Great! You now have an object that follows a path and rotates to face forward as it moves.

A second method to make an object follow a path is the *ClampTo* method. This method does not turn an object to face forward as it moves, however. It's especially useful if you need to control your object using a *Driver* or a physical force but need the object's motion constrained to the path. To use this method, select your object, and from the *Constraints* tab, add a *ClampTo* constraint. ▶6.17

6.16

Then choose the *Curve* object from the *Target* field. Once it is added, you can move, rotate, and scale your object as usual. When you do this, however, the object's position in *X*, *Y*, and *Z* will always be constrained (clamped) to fall on the curve. ▶6.18

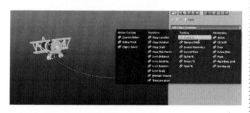

6.17

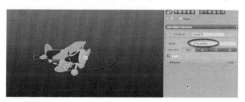

6.18

6.3 Curves and Colors

Splines and paths make useful control objects for animation. They're used frequently for building motion paths, for acting like bones, and for working with inverse kinematics, among others. For this reason, splines are used widely in animation. However, by default, the visibility of splines in the viewport can be awkward. They can be difficult to see properly when deselected, and they're all displayed in the same color. You can, however, customize this. ▶6.19

6.19

6.20

To make a curve thicker and more prominent in the viewport, select the curve, and switch to the *Curve* tab in the Properties panel. From there, increase the *Depth* field. This assigns the curve a thickness, generating a mesh along the curve. ▶6.20

Next, from the *Shape* rollout in the *Curve* tab of the Properties panel, select *Full* for the *Fill type*. This allows the curve faces to render from all angles. ▶6.21

6.21

6.22

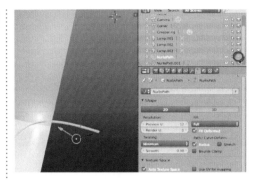

Now deactivate the renderability of the curve from the Outliner to prevent the faces and thickness from displaying in renders. To achieve this, simply deactivate the render icon from the Outliner. ▶**6.22**

It's helpful to customize the curve appearance by using custom colors. This lets you change how curves look, giving each curve a unique appearance that is meaningful to your animation workflow. To do this, you can assign the curve a material. Using the Blender render engine, just switch to the *Materials* tab from the Properties panel, and assign the curve a new material. Click the + icon to add a material slot, and then click the *New* button to create a new material for the selected spline. ▶**6.23**

6.23

6.24

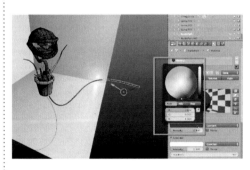

Assign the material a color from the *Diffuse* slot in the *Materials* tab. This determines the color of the spline in the viewport. ▶**6.24**

By default, the material is affected by scene lighting. To make the curve color more vibrant and eye-catching in the viewport, activate the *Shadeless* option for the material. ▶6.25

6.25

Voila! You can now customize curve appearance in the viewport. ▶6.26

6.26

6.4 Animation Baking

Blender supports many types of procedural animation, like motion paths and physical simulations. With motion paths, we can draw a curve and have an object follow it. With physical simulations, we can adjust the initial variables and conditions and then see how objects unfold and behave according to the physical forces. These animation types and others are calculated, sometimes on a per-frame basis and sometimes in batches, based on specific inputs, like splines and formulas. These types of animation allow for parametric flexibility; that is, you can change them and the outcome by adjusting type-in properties directly from the Properties panel. This makes such animations easy to tweak

6.27

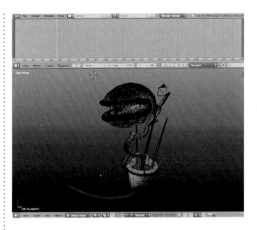

and change. But it also means that they are not fundamentally key frame based, insofar as they don't produce tangible and editable key frames in the Animation Timeline. ▶6.27

Animations lacking definition through key frames are problematic, especially if they are to be exported successfully to other applications, like game engines (e.g., Unity or Unreal). Features and capabilities differ between animation software, and many applications only support imported animations based on key frames. For this reason, it's important to be able to convert animations in Blender into key frames where needed, which is known as *animation baking*. ▶6.28

6.28

Let's consider an example of animation baking to detail the procedure. Take a path animation: an airplane traveling along a spline path, as considered earlier in the chapter, using the *Follow Path* constraint. It moves from one side of the path to the other over time by keyframing the *Evaluation Time* field of the curve on the first and last frames, from *0* to *100*. This animation produces no key frames for the airplane object that moves, even though it flies across the path throughout the animation. ▶**6.29**

You can, however, bake the animation of the plane to key frames. This converts the animation into key frames, and it removes the dependency of the plane on the curve object. This is because, after the bake, the key frames define the motion of the plane and not the curve. To do this, select the airplane object (or the object for key frame baking), and then choose *Object > Animation > Bake Action* from the 3D menu. ▶**6.30**

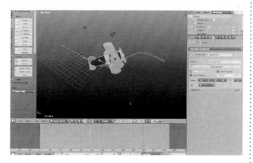

6.29

6.30

Selecting *Bake Action* displays the Bake menu, offering control and customization of how the bake is saved to key frames. Unfortunately, the Bake menu is not resizable and does not display the full names of all options. The options, from top to bottom, are *Only Selected Objects*, *Visual Keyframe*, *Clear Constraints*, *Clear Parents*, and *Overwrite*. ▶**6.31**

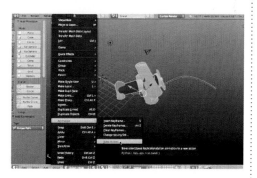

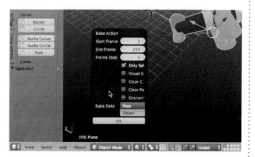

6.31

To bake key frames, activate all check boxes. Specify the animation range using the *Start Frame* and *End Frame* fields. The *Frame Step* field specifies the interval of frames for which a key frame should be made. This value varies depending on the animation being baked. This value should be lower for animations with rapid change and higher for smoother and longer animations. The default value of *1* means a key frame is generated for every frame. This offers the greatest accuracy and preservation but could result in the production of many unnecessary key frames. This can lead to messy results and poor performance for real-time game engines. ▶6.32

6.32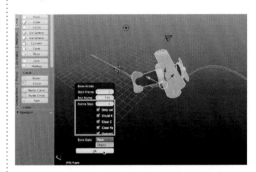

6.33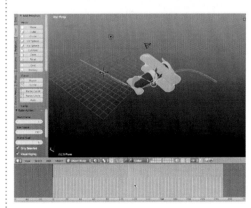

Ideally, *Frame Step* should be as high as possible while achieving the results you need. On clicking *OK*, the animation will be baked to key frames. For longer, complex animations, this may take a few minutes or more. Once completed, the results will be evident in the Animation Timeline as new key frames are generated for the selected object. ▶6.33

6.34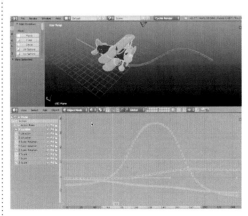

After generating key frames, you'll probably want to check out key frame interpolation inside the Graph Editor, to ensure the animation maintains its original pacing. Nothing may need to be done, but in some cases some minor tweaks to the curves may be required. ▶6.34

If you need to export your animated objects to other applications and game engines, you can choose *File > Export*. For animation, the *DAE* and the *FBX* formats are widely supported options. ▶6.35

6.35

6.5 Squash and Stretch

"Squash and stretch" is a fundamental principle of animation that describes the elastic characteristic of many objects, making them change shape slightly during motion. And even with solids that don't change shape, the effect can still be used to emphasize motion, drama, and mood. Blender offers a relatively straightforward method for creating this effect. Select your object, which should squash and stretch, and then add a *Maintain Volume* constraint, available from the *Constraint* tab in the *Properties* window. ▶6.36

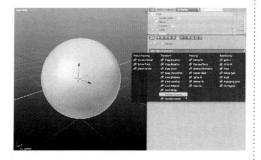

6.36

The *Maintain Volume* constraint applies scale compensation to an object automatically along a specified axis to maintain its initial volume. Thus, by scaling the object, Blender automatically adjusts object size in the remaining dimensions to maintain a consistent volume overall. Use the *Free* setting to specify the axis on which free scaling may occur. For a simple squash-and-stretch ball scenario, this will likely be the *Z* axis. ▶6.37

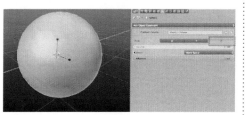

6.37

151

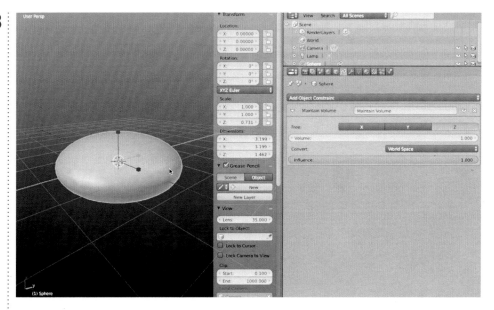

6.38

Once specified, try scaling the object on the free axis. When you do this, the object changes shape across the remaining dimensions. This can be used to create a squash-and-stretch effect when scale is keyframed over time. ▶6.38

6.6 Hierarchical Rigging

Remember, object hierarchies in Blender are especially important for animation. Objects in a scene exist in a hierarchy where objects relate to one another. An object can be a parent, sibling, or child based on its relationship to another object. A parent is a top-level object that can have no, one, or more children. A child object is a lower order object to a parent. Siblings refer to multiple child objects with the same parent. ▶6.39

6.39

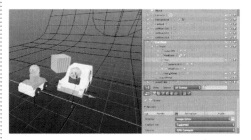

Hierarchies are, essentially, a form of rigging because the relationship between objects defines how they transform. Transformations cascade downward in a hierarchy. This means that when a parent object is moved, rotated, or scaled, all child objects will be transformed too to maintain their relative offset from the parent object. For this reason, if you're making a car object with passengers inside, you'll want to make sure the passengers are child objects of the car body. As the car moves, the passengers should move with it. This principle applies to airplanes, trains, ships, or any objects that depend on another. You can encode this relationship with hierarchies—just by dragging and dropping objects onto each inside the Outliner window in Blender. More information on the Outliner window can be found online at https://www.blender.org/manual/editors/outliner.html. ▶6.40

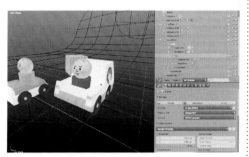

6.40

6.7 Selection Controls

Some objects consist of complex hierarchies with many levels of nesting—children within children, and so on. When working with animations on many objects like this, it can be difficult selecting things in the viewport, getting exactly the object you need, as opposed to a parent or child or related object. You can accidentally pick a child object instead of a parent, or vice versa. In addition, you may want to animate the objects but not associate key frames with any particular one. You can solve these problems using *Selection Controls*: This is about creating a dummy object that stands in for the hierarchy and controls all children automatically. ▶6.41

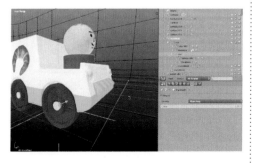

6.41

6.42

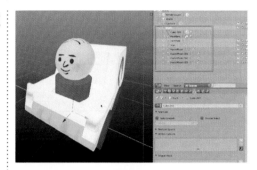

Let's see this process in action. Consider a scene in which a truck object is the parent of many others, such as the passenger, the wheels, and more. When the truck is transformed, everything associated with it also transforms, via cascading transformations. ▶6.42

6.43

Rather than select any specific object in the truck to create an animation, we can use a control object instead. Let's create a control object by switching to the *Create* panel and creating an empty object. Simply click the *Empty* button. ▶6.43

6.44

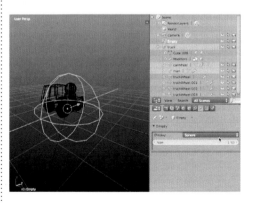

After creating an empty, change its viewport avatar via the *Properties* window. Switch to the *Empty Data* tab, and change the *Display* field from *Plain Axes* to *Sphere*. Change the size to something that encompasses your model hierarchy. This makes the empty gizmo easier to see and select. ▶6.44

Rename the empty to root_Car—or whatever is appropriate for your object. I use the prefix *root* to indicate that it's the ultimate parent object. ▶6.45

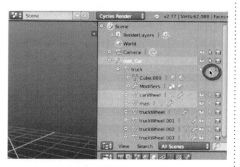

6.45

Next, use the Outliner panel to drag and drop your object hierarchy (for me, the car object) under the empty, making the empty a parent object. ▶6.46

6.46

Now make all objects in the hierarchy, except for the root empty object, nonselectable. You can do this in one operation by holding down the *Ctrl* key and clicking the selectable icon for the object hierarchy at the root level. This toggles the selectability for objects down the hierarchy. Once this is completed, the only selectable object in the hierarchy should be the empty root object. ▶6.47

6.47

Excellent work! Now you can select the complete object by one click in the viewport on the empty gizmo. This transforms all objects in the hierarchy, and you cannot accidentally select any of the child objects. ▶6.48

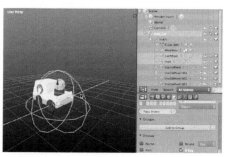

6.48

6.8 Hooks

You'll often need to animate parts of objects rather than whole objects, like the petals of a flower or the expressions on a character face. In these instances, you need to animate the vertices *within* a mesh, instead of the *complete* mesh with all the vertices. You can do this using *armatures*, but you can also use *hooks*, which are simpler to use and can be effective for simple subobject changes—like objects that must bend, twist, or flex. Let's see how to use hooks in a specific case: for the Suzanne monkey head, to change its expression. Open up a new scene, create a monkey head, and apply a subdivision surface modifier to increase its smoothness. ▶6.49

6.49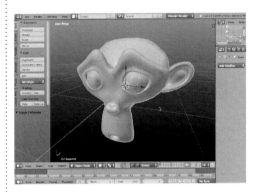

Next, select the top vertices of the eye section in the model. By raising and lowering these vertices, with falloff, you can create surprised, shocked, tired, or bored facial expressions. ▶6.50

6.50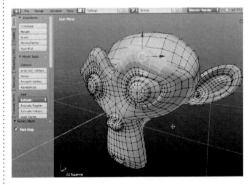

With the vertices selected, choose *Mesh > Vertices > Hooks > Hook to New Object* from the 3D menu. Choosing this option creates a new, empty object in the scene and applies an auto-configured *Hook* modifier to the monkey mesh. The newly created empty is a special hook object that's associated with the selected vertices. ▶6.51

6.51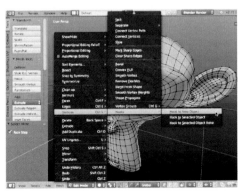

After creating the hook object, select it, and switch to the *Empty Data* tab. From there, use the *Display* drop-down to change the visibility, size, and shape of the viewport gizmo to better represent the area it affects within the monkey mesh. In my case, I've used a *Sphere* gizmo with a size of *0.20*. ▶6.52

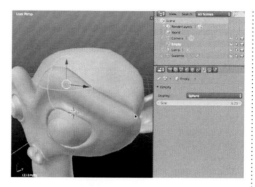

Next, by moving the hook object, you transform the associated vertices in the monkey mesh. What's great about this is that the hook object can be animated. Therefore, you get animate-able control over an object's vertices at the object level. ▶6.53

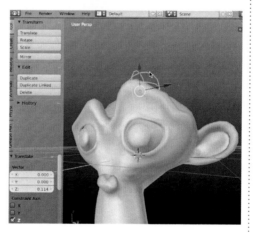

Repeat this process for the vertices over the other eye in the monkey model, which allows you to create symmetrical and asymmetrical effects. Then, name the hook objects appropriately, such as hook_LeftEye and hook_RightEye. ▶6.54

You can also control the falloff effect of a hook over the range of its associated vertices by selecting the original mesh (the monkey head) and tweaking the *Radius* field for the *Hook* modifier. Remember, if you add two hooks, there will be two modifiers, one for each hook.

6.55

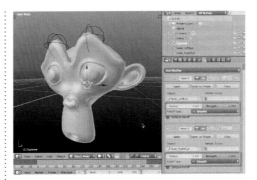

Falloff Type is used to control the shape of the falloff interpolation between the vertices, across the *Radius*. ▶6.55

6.56

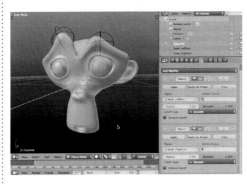

By translating, rotating, and scaling hooks, you can pose and control a mesh and its vertices—even in animation. Thus, hooks give you similar subobject-level control of a mesh to that provided by armatures. Armatures offer more extensive control and flexibility than hooks, but the simplicity of hooks makes them an ideal choice for straightforward morphs and poses. ▶6.56

6.9 Grease Pencil Referencing and Animation

The Grease Pencil is a drawing tool built into Blender that lets you make diagnostic brushstrokes directly within the viewport. It's especially useful for drawing out trajectories, paths, wireframes, and other reference lines and shapes that are used

6.57

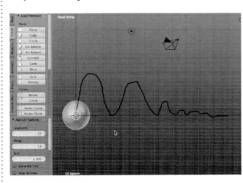

in animation. Grease Pencil strokes are not typically rendered or included in a final animation, but they are used to guide animators in the animating process. A classic example is a Grease Pencil stroke representing the bouncing ball trajectory. This outlines the path a bouncing ball should take throughout an animation. ▶6.57

Here's how to use the Grease Pencil. Display the N Panel by pressing *N* on the keyboard, and view the *Grease Pencil* rollout. From there, click *New Layer* to create a new, empty Grease Pencil layer. This works like a Photoshop layer. All brushstrokes are applied to the selected layer. ▶6.58

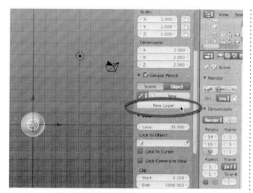

6.58

With the Grease Pencil layer created, expand the Tools panel, and open the *Grease Pencil* tab. This tab lets you create new brushstrokes and erase existing ones if needed. Activate the options *Additive Drawing* and *Continuous Drawing*. *Additive Drawing* lets you *add* brushstrokes to any existing strokes, like a regular brush, instead of replacing existing strokes. *Continuous Drawing* lets you lay down strokes by clicking your mouse, and the drawing mode continues until you explicitly press the *Esc* key on the keyboard. ▶6.59

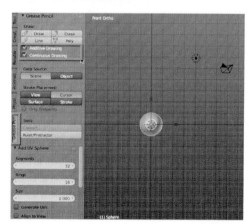

6.59

To make a new brushstroke using either the mouse or the pen tablet, click the *Draw* button from the *Grease Pencil* tab in the Tools panel. Or you can press and hold the keyboard shortcut *D* for the duration of the stroke. ▶6.60

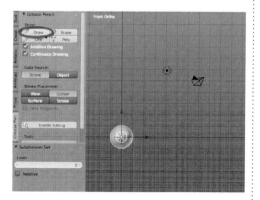

6.60

6.61

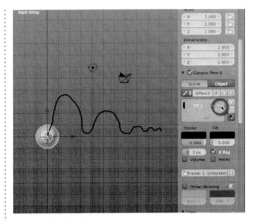

6.62

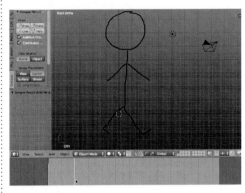

6.63

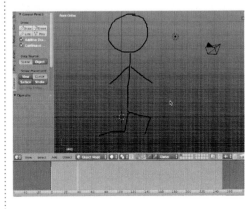

Once drawn, you can toggle layer visibility from the N Panel by clicking the layer eye icon. This hides or shows the brushstrokes. ▶6.61

One of the amazing features and properties of the Grease Pencil is that it can be animated! That is, the state of a Grease Pencil layer in any frame is keyframed. This means a Grease Pencil layer can look different between frames, allowing you to create *animation references* as opposed to static frame references. To work with Grease Pencil animation, simply move the timeline slider to the relevant position in the *Timeline* window, and then start drawing with the Grease Pencil! ▶6.62

Then just move to the next frame, and start drawing again! Now, when you scrub the timeline, moving from frame to frame, the Grease Pencil sketch changes to show the relevant strokes. This is really useful for creating character pose references and lines of action. ▶6.63

6.10 *Rigify*

Animators frequently need to create animated characters. To make this possible, armatures are needed to approximate the limbs and structure of a character for animation. You can manually build an armature, but Blender offers the *Rigify* add-on for generating readymade character rigs. ▶6.64

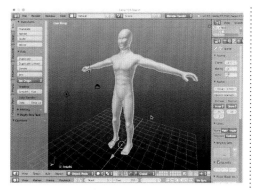

6.64

To activate the *Rigify* add-on, access the *User Preferences* window by choosing *File > User Preferences* from the application menu. Switch to the *Add-ons* tab, and search for *rigify*. Then enable that option to activate the *Rigify* add-on. ▶6.65

6.65

When *Rigify* is activated, you can quickly and easily generate a new character rig by selecting *Add > Armature > Human (Meta-Rig)*. You also have a more complex armature available through *Add > Armature > Pitchipoy Human (Meta-Rig)*. ▶6.66

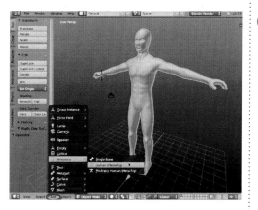

6.66

6.67

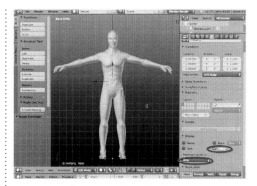

After adding a character rig to the scene, you may need to re-pose it to fit the pose and shape of your existing character model before starting the rigging process. You can also change the visibility of the rig using the *Object Data* tab. Enable *X-Ray* to always see the rig on top of your model, and enable *Wire* to see the rig in wireframe mode. ▶**6.67**

6.68

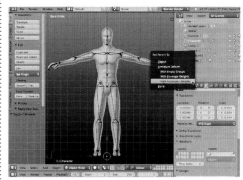

When you're ready to rig your character, drag and drop the character mesh in the Outliner onto the *Rigify* rig. Then choose *Armature Deform With Automatic Weights* from the context menu. This lets Blender auto-configure the mesh to the rig, creating vertex groups, and it usually works very well. ▶**6.68**

6.69

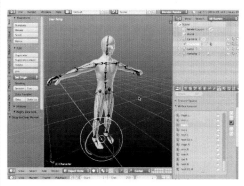

After this, Blender generates a vertex group for each limb and body part, and these are weighted to specific bones in the armature. When the armature changes in *Pose* mode, it has implications for the character mesh. This makes bone deformation possible. ▶**6.69**

NOTE

Rigs generated with *Rigify* do not always translate well to humanoid game engine rigs. Some engines offer advice on how to convert *Rigify* rigs for game engine import (e.g., https://docs.unity3d.com/Manual/BlenderAndRigify.html)

7

Rendering Cheats

Rendering is about making beautiful stills and animations. It's about transforming your scene from a rough, working project into a final, fully produced form. The output from a render will typically be a still image file, like a PNG file, or a fully rendered animation video, like an MP4 file. The Render process, however, poses many challenges. The most significant one is that of time; specifically, renders can take a long time. And I mean a long time! From minutes and hours to days and even weeks! This chapter explores some tips and tricks for reducing render times, ways to optimize renders, and things to improve. In addition, it'll explore other rendering issues too: how to make your renders prettier and how to achieve more unconventional renders. Let's see these.

Rendering Cheats

7.1 Rendering Wireframes

When developing your portfolio, you'll often want to show a mode's wireframe in a render—that is, to show the faces, edge loops, and general topology of a model,

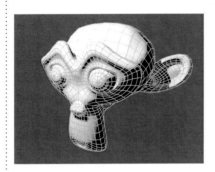

demonstrating how it's been constructed in terms of polygons. Showing this information is helpful to other artists. It shows how cleanly you work and how effectively you build models. In addition, it can lead to some very interesting visual styles too. ▶7.1

To render a wireframe for any model, start by selecting the model, and switch to the *Modifiers* tab in the *Properties* window. Then add a *Wireframe* modifier. ▶7.2

7.1

7.2

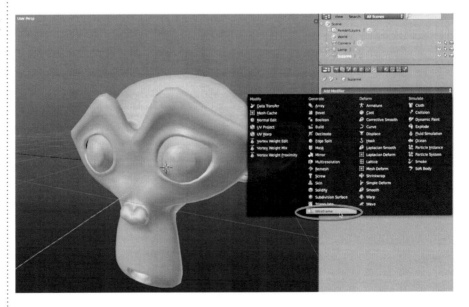

When applied to the model, the *Wireframe* modifier automatically replaces the original mesh with newly generated geometry, representing all edge loops.

You'll want to change this by deactivating the *Replace Original* check box. This restores the original geometry *and* generates a wireframe on top. ▶7.3

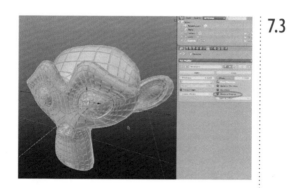

By default, the wireframe is assigned the first material attached to the object, whether you're using Blender Internal or Blender Render. You'll probably want to assign the wireframe a different and unique material. In the Blender Render engine, the wireframe material should be marked with *Shadeless*, and in Blender Cycles, you use an *Emission Shader* to replicate the same behavior. ▶7.4

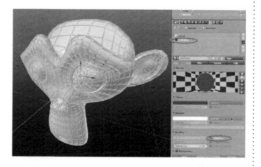

You can assign the *Wireframe* modifier any material you want by using the *Material Offset* field. This defines a numerical index of the material to use: Starting at *0.0* indicates that the topmost (first) material in the material list should be applied to the wireframe, *1* indicates the next material, *2* the next, and so on. For an object that has two materials, the first for the object itself and the second for the wireframe part, the *Material Offset* should be *1*. ▶7.5

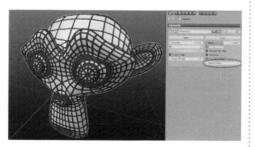

Finally, you can tweak the thickness and extension of the wireframe by using both the *Thickness* field and the Offset *field*, respectively. Thickness controls

7.6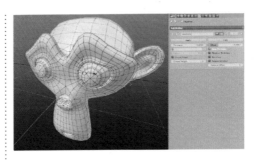

the radius of each wire in the wireframe, and offset controls how extruded the wireframe is from the mesh. ▶7.6

Excellent! You can now render models in *Wireframe* mode. Click *Render*, and you're done.

7.2 Texture Baking

Rendering is not just about producing fancy shots of your scene from specific camera angles, whether for still shots or animations. You can configure the renderer to output pixel data to an object's texture via its UV mapping. This is especially useful for games and simulations, but it's also useful for creating a scene where objects can be examined and previewed in real time without having to rely on a render engine. *Texture baking* lets you save the complete rendered result of an object to a texture. This means you can easily map the texture onto

7.7

the object to make it look illuminated and accurately rendered in real time. Let's see how this works. ▶7.7

Begin with a Blender scene (an example can be downloaded for free from Blend Swap at http://www. blendswap.com/blends/view/56197). To start the texture-baking process, make sure your objects have UV

7.8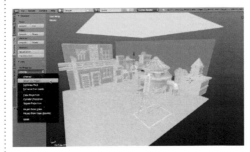

mapping applied *with no overlapping UVs*. You can create this kind of layout with Smart UV Project. For texture baking, it's important that your objects don't have overlapping UVs, as each part of your mesh needs to map to its own pixels in the texture. ▶7.8

To bake with *Cycles*, create a new texture inside the UV Image Editor. To do this, select *Image > New Image* from the UV Image Editor menu. This texture will contain all the baked pixels. ▶**7.9**

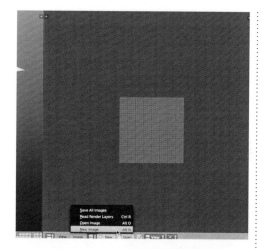

7.9

The newly created texture can be of any appropriate size, it doesn't need an alpha channel, and it can be filled with black. An appropriate size depends on your needs. Larger sizes should be used for complete environments seen close in first-person perspective. ▶**7.10**

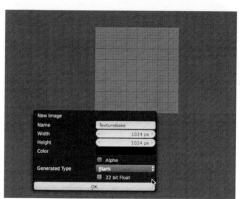

7.10

Next, switch to the Node Editor Window to view your object's material configuration. Then create a new *Texture* node. To do this, select *Add > Texture > Image Texture* from the UV Image Editor menu. This creates a new *Texture* node in the graph. ▶**7.11**

After creating a *Texture* node, use the *Texture* picker to select the newly created texture, in order to associate the texture to the node. Finally, click the node to select it, if it's not already selected. A bold border should be drawn around the node perimeter, indicating its

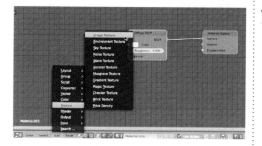

7.11

7.12

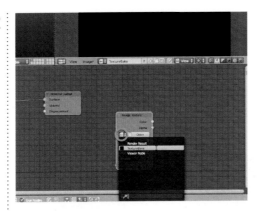

7.13

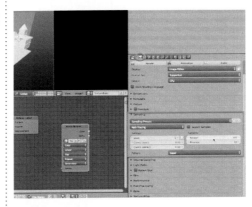

7.14

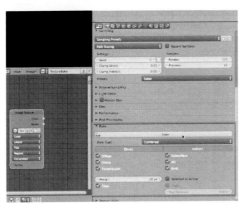

selected status. Selecting the texture node is important for later, as it specifies the target texture for bake output. ▶7.12

Now we're ready to start texture baking! Select the model to bake, and access the *Render* tab from the *Properties* window. Expand the *Samples* rollout, and specify a maximum setting for the *Render Samples*. In short, the higher this value, the more polished, detailed, and refined your render will look, but at the cost of render time. You'll need to find a balance that works best for your scene. ▶7.13

Then expand the *Bake* rollout. From the *Bake Type* drop-down, select *Combined*. On selecting *Combined*, everything in the scene will be rendered and then baked—including all *Diffuse*, *Bump*, and *Specular* information— as one single, texture map. Then click the button *Bake*. This initiates the *Bake* process, which may take a while depending on your scene and hardware. ▶7.14

Once everything is baked, the UV Image Editor displays the final texture. This should be saved *with Image > Save Image* from the Image Editor menu. ▶**7.15**

Finally, you can assign the baked texture as the *Diffuse* channel of the object's material. When you do this, the object immediately appears as it does in a render, directly in the viewport! ▶**7.16**

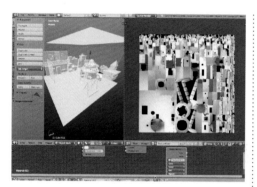

7.15

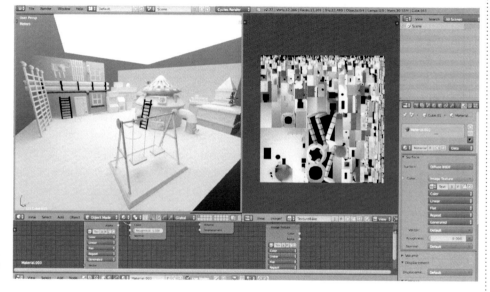

7.16

7.3 Progressive Refine

The Cycles Render engine is powerful and capable of highly realistic results. The *Sampling* rollout from the *Render* tab is used to control the maximum quality achievable in a render. Effectively, the *Render* field, under the *Samples* section, controls how many steps or stages of refinement the Cycles renderer must

7.17

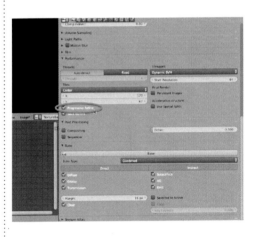

7.18

complete on the image before ending the render. Higher values result in smoother, more polished renders with less noise. This comes at the cost of time, however. Higher sampled renders take longer to produce. ▶7.17

To produce a render, you'll typically fill in the *Render Samples* field and then click *Render*. The problem with this standard approach, however, is that if *Render Samples* is too low, the render will look too noisy, and if *Render Samples* is too high, then the renderer wastes time producing unnecessary refinement. Ideally, you can set *Render Samples* to exactly the value you need before rendering, but often you don't know what the value should be. Sometimes, then, it's preferable to just have Blender continue rendering until it looks right, in your judgment, and then you can tell it to stop manually.

You can achieve this using *Progressive Refine*. This technique, when enabled, is often slower than a conventional render, but it saves you from wasting time producing renders with inappropriate *Render Samples*. To activate *Progressive Refine*, expand the *Performance* rollout on the *Render* tab, and then activate the *Progressive Refine* check box. ▶7.18

Even when *Progressive Refine* is activated, Cycles only continues rendering for as far as the *Render Samples* field specifies. For this reason, when *Progressive Refine* is activated, you'll typically set the *Render Samples* to the highest value expected, as you can always terminate the render earlier if needed. Therefore, return to the

Sampling rollout in the *Render* tab, and specify a higher value for the *Render Samples.* ▶7.19

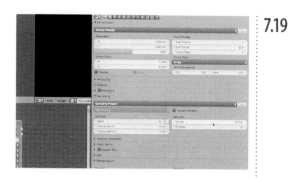

Finally, press *Render,* and the render begins. With *Progressive Render* enabled, Cycles avoids using bucket rendering (tiles rendering), in which square, grid-aligned blocks of the image are rendered one at a time. Instead, the entire image is progressively rendered over time. When you're happy with the render quality, simply press *Esc* to terminate the render, and you're left with your final image inside the UV Image Editor. ▶7.20

7.4 Tiles and Bounces

By default, Cycles is configured to render at a very high quality. This is likely to create long render times for larger and complex scenes. You can, however, substantially tweak the settings to reduce render times without sacrificing notable quality. Specifically, the *Performance* and *Light Paths* settings can be optimized. ▶7.21

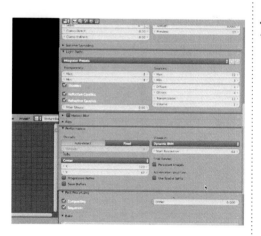

The *Bounces* section of the *Light Paths* rollout controls how many times light can bounce around the scene. Every intersection between an incident ray of light and an

7.22

7.23

object counts as a bounce. The default *Maximum* is normally far too high. A value of *4* normally produces very similar results at much better speeds. So change this to *4*, and see how it works for you. Repeat this for the other fields too, such as *Diffuse*, *Glossy*, *Transmission*, and *Volume*. ▶7.22

For the *Performance* rollout, take special care about the render tile size for *X* and *Y*. This refers to the pixel dimensions of a single tile (section of image) that is continuously produced by Cycles when *Progressive Render* is not activated. The size and dimensions of tiles can influence the render speed. When sizing tiles, use *Power-2* sizes as these are demonstrably faster—that is, sizes of *16*, *32*, *64*, *128*, *256*, and *512*. For GPU rendering, larger sizes can be used for greater effectiveness. ▶7.23

7.5 Render Selections

Renders can take a long time, and sometimes when making a small tweak to a scene, you don't want to re-render the whole image just to see the effect of your new changes. Instead, you just want to render a *relevant section* of the larger

7.24

image. This significantly reduces render time and lets you preview only the relevant changes. Blender lets you do this with *Render Borders*. To activate this feature, convert your viewport into Camera View by choosing *View > Camera* from the 3D menu. This lets you see the viewport from the perspective of the render camera. ▶7.24

Next, draw a render border in the viewport, representing the rectangle to render. Areas outside the rectangle will not be rendered. To do this, select *View > Render Border* from the 3D menu. You can then click and drag a box selection in the viewport to draw the render border. ▶7.25

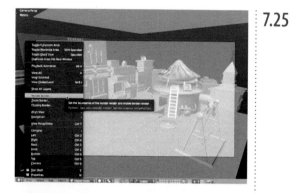

7.25

Once drawn, the render border appears as a red boundary in the viewport, indicating the renderable region—that is, the region to be rendered when you click *Render.* ▶7.26

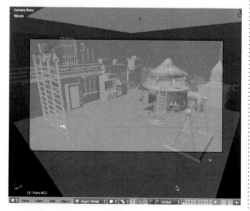

7.26

When you click *Render* from the *Properties* window, the region is rendered. Areas outside the border appear in black. ▶7.27

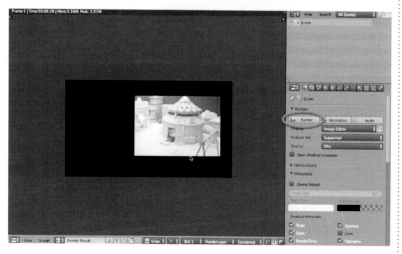

7.27

7.28

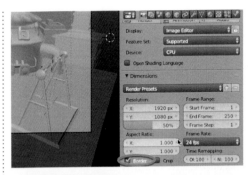

7.29

7.30

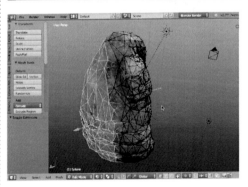

If your render is not constrained within the border or if the border doesn't show up in the viewport, make sure the *Border* option is activated in the *Dimensions* rollout of the *Render* tab, in the *Properties* window. ▶7.28

To clear the render border, access the space bar menu by pressing the *Space Bar* key on the keyboard, and type *Clear Render Border* into the *Search* field. Then click the *Clear Render Border* option from the menu. This clears the render border, enabling a full-screen render again. ▶7.29

7.6 Manual Culling

Render calculations are based on scene data: The more lights, models, and effects in the scene, the more complex the render calculation. You can improve render time by simplifying the scene. One way to achieve this is by deleting the faces of a model that are not directly visible to the render camera. This method is most effective for still renders but not for animations. ▶7.30

7.7 Comparative Renders

You'll often create multiple renders of a scene for testing lighting, colors, angles, and details, checking to see which renders you prefer. To make decisions about which renders should be accepted and which discarded, you'll want to make easy and quick comparisons. You can do this easily directly from the UV Image Editor, using the *Slots* feature. To get started, create an initial render of your scene by clicking the *Render* button from the Properties panel. ▶7.31

7.31

When completed, your render appears in the UV Image Editor. By default, your first render is assigned to *Slot 1*. This is displayed inside the Image Editor, from the bottom toolbar. ▶7.32

7.32

You can now switch to *Slot 2* and create a new, second render with your adjustments applied. To do this, just select *Slot 2* from the *Slot* drop-down list in the UV Image Editor toolbar. When the render is completed, the result will be output to *Slot 2*. ▶7.33

That's it! You can now easily compare renders by selecting different slots from the UV Image Editor. By selecting *Slot 1*, you'll view the associated render, and so on. This offers you an effective means of quickly and easily flicking between slots to see the associated renders. Blender offers a total of eight render slots.

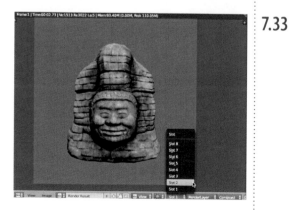

7.33

7.8 Render Layers

One especially important method for simplifying renders, and to reduce render times, is to use *render layers*. Render layers let you group related objects in a scene such that, when the scene is rendered, the objects are rendered together on a separate layer. This offers benefits in addition to simplicity and optimization. Render layers give you more control over a render. By rendering related objects to separate layers, you gain additional postprocess and compositing control. You can add effects to specific layers, change blending modes, apply differential render effects, and more. ▶7.34

7.34

To get started using render layers, using an example of two render layers, select your foreground objects, and move them to a new layer in the scene. These objects should render separately. To achieve this, select the foreground objects, and press *M* on the keyboard, or choose *Object > Move to Layer* from the 3D menu. ▶7.35

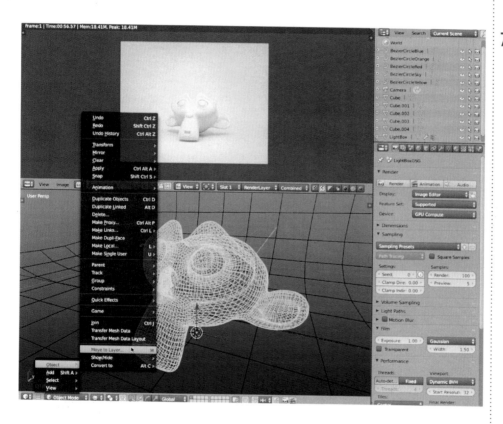

7.35

Next, choose an available layer for the object from the *Layer Select* menu, simply by clicking on it. Available layers appear as empty boxes in the menu, while occupied layers display a center dot icon. Once the layer is chosen, the selected

7.36

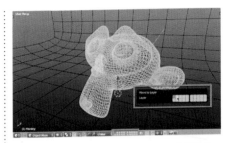

7.37

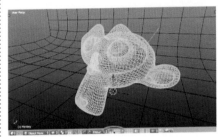

7.38

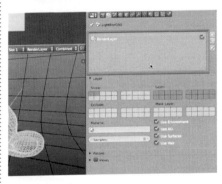

7.39

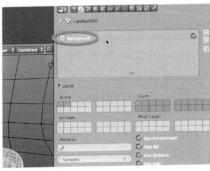

objects will move to the chosen layer in the scene. ▶7.36

The selected objects disappear in the viewport, having now moved to a new layer. You can easily see all the contents of a layer in the viewport by clicking its layer icon from the 3D toolbar. In addition, you can see multiple layers simultaneously by *Shift*-clicking the layers instead. ▶7.37

After dividing and organizing objects over layers in the scene, you're ready to use render layers. The options and behavior of render layers differ between the Internal and Cycles renderers. Here, we'll consider Cycles. Switch to the *Render Layers* tab in the *Properties* window. By default, there will be one render layer. From this panel, you can view a list of all render layers and the properties of the selected layer. ▶7.38

Rename the initial render layer as "Background." This will contain only the background objects on the first scene layer. To do this, double-click the render layer name in the *Render Layer* list. Then enter a new name for the layer, and press *Enter* to confirm. ▶7.39

Now create a second render layer, and rename it as "Foreground." New layers are added by clicking the + icon from the *Render Layers* list. ▶**7.40**

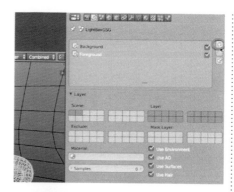

7.40

Select the layer named *Background* from the *Render Layer* list, and its properties and options will appear in the interface below. For the *Layer* field, you can select all *scene layers* associated with this render layer. That is, all objects on the associated scene layers will render a single, consolidated render layer. By default, all scene layers are associated with a newly created render layer. You can click specific scene layers to dissociate them. For the *Background* layer, only the first scene layer should be selected. ▶**7.41**

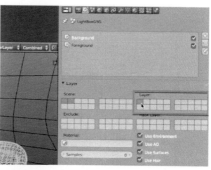

7.41

Now select the render layer named *Foreground*, and associate this with the *Foreground* scene layer. All objects attached to that layer become linked with the render layer. ▶**7.42**

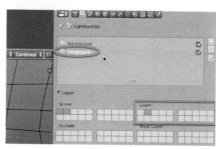

7.42

On rendering the scene now, your render results will look very different. Rendering occurs in two steps instead of one, one step for each render layer. It also produces two separate images, one for the *Foreground* and one for the *Background*. In the UV Image Editor, you can view each render layer separately by choosing its name from the *Layer Selection* drop-down. ▶**7.43**

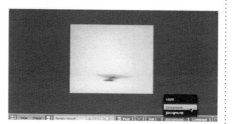

7.43

7.44

7.45

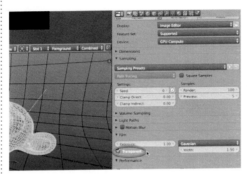

7.46

One problem that pops up for the *Foreground* layer is that it renders with a bold color for the background, as opposed to transparency. You'll often want render layers to output with transparent backgrounds, making them easier to manipulate and composite in photo-editing software, like Photoshop. You'll often want to stack up render layers in an image composition. ▶7.44

To enable transparency for render layers, switch to the *Render* tab in the *Properties* window. Then expand the *Film* rollout. From here, enable the *Transparent* check box to support transparent backgrounds. ▶7.45

Finally, expand the *Output* rollout from the *Render* tab, and activate the *RGBA* color option, to support an *Alpha* component for rendered colors. ▶7.46

Now re-render the scene, and your render layers will have transparent backgrounds wherever there is no geometry to render. You can save the render layers to an image file, complete with transparency, by choosing *Image > Save Image* for each render layer from the UV Image Editor menu.

7.9 Render Layers and Image Files

If you render job features lots of render layers, it can be tedious having to save every layer as a separate image individually using the UV Image Editor.

This is especially true if you're producing multiple render jobs. Ideally, Blender should be able to save all render layers to separate files after the render is completed. And thankfully, Blender can do this! Let's see how. First, open up a scene with multiple render layers configured. Then, switch to the *Render* tab from the *Properties* window. Expand the *Post Processing* rollout, and activate the *Compositing* check box. This instructs Blender to run all rendered output through the compositing nodes, if any exist. ►7.47

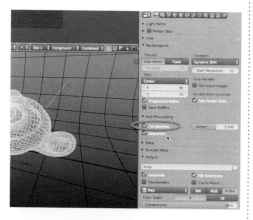

7.47

Next, open the Node Editor in the interface, and activate the compositing nodes. To do this, select the *Compositing Nodes* icon from the Node Editor toolbar, and click the *Use Nodes* check box. ►7.48

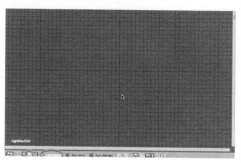

7.48

Now we can use the Node Editor to connect our render layers to file-saving nodes. To get started, click *Add > Input > Render Layers* from the Node Editor menu. When you do this, a new *Render Layer* node is created in the graph. ►7.49

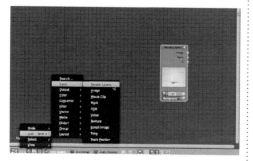

7.49

7.50

From the *Render Layer* node, click the *Layer Select* drop-down to choose the render layer associated with the node. ▶7.50

7.51

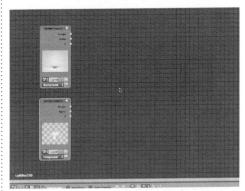

Repeat this process, adding a new render layer node to graph for each render layer in the scene. ▶7.51

7.52

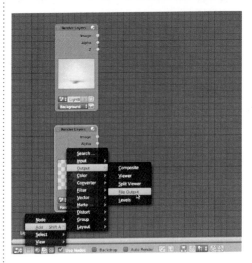

Next, we'll add a new *File Output* node. This accepts image data as input (e.g., from a *Render Layer* node) and then outputs them to an image file. To add this, click *Add > Output > File Output*. ▶7.52

Once it is added, connect the output socket of a *Render Layer* node to the input socket of the *File Output* node. ▶**7.53**

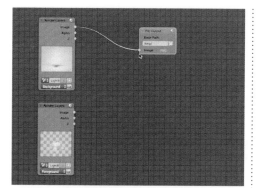

7.53

You can configure *File Output* options by displaying the Node Editor N Panel (by pressing the *N* key on the keyboard) and then selecting the *File Output* node in the graph. From the options, assign the file output a file name, and choose the PNG format in *RGBA* color mode to preserve transparency. ▶**7.54**

7.54

Next, duplicate the *File Output* node, changing the file name for each duplicate, and connect these to the corresponding render layer nodes. At this point, each render layer should be connected to a unique *File Output* node, saving to a unique file. ▶**7.55**

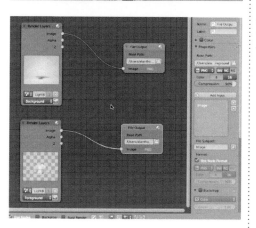

7.55

7.56

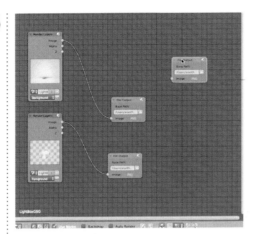

Finally, return to the 3D view, and press *Render* from the *Render* tab in the *Properties* window. This initiates and performs the render process. On completion, the compositor graph will generate unique image files, with transparency included, for each render layer. ▶7.56

7.10 Combining Render Layers

Being able to separate objects into unique render layers is great for organizing and streamlining your render process. But you'll also want to consolidate layers and combine them together, producing both layered and combined renders. You could achieve this by rendering twice—once by using render layers and otherwise by rendering everything on one layer. But you don't need to do that. Following on from the previous tip, you can tweak the *File Output* node setup to output a consolidated layer, simply based on the two separate render layers. Let's see how. Start by creating an additional *File Output* node to save the consolidated image data to a file. ▶7.57

7.57

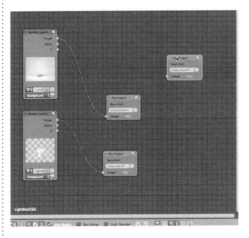

Next, create an *Alpha Over* node by selecting *Add > Color > Alpha Over* from the Node Editor menu. This node accepts two image inputs with alpha channels and overlays one image atop the other, allowing for transparency of the top layer. It outputs the consolidated result. ▶7.58

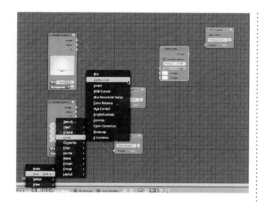

7.58

Now connect your existing render layer nodes into the image connections of the *Alpha Over* node. The top connection represents the top layer, and the bottom connection represents the bottom layer. Then, connect the *Alpha Over* node output to the *File Output* node. This configuration combines all render layers as inputs and then outputs a consolidated result through the *File Output* node. ▶7.59

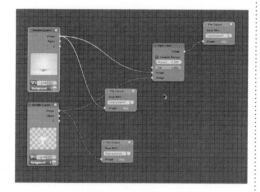

7.59

If you've completed a render previously, Blender can show you a real-time preview from the combined *Alpha* node. To do this, enable the *Backdrop* checkbox from the Node Editor toolbar. ▶7.60

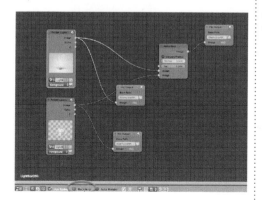

7.60

Then add a *Viewer* node by choosing *Add > Output > Viewer* from the Node Editor menu. Then connect the *Alpha Over* output to the *Viewer* node. When you do this, you'll see a preview as a backdrop for the Node Editor. Great work! ▶7.61

7.61

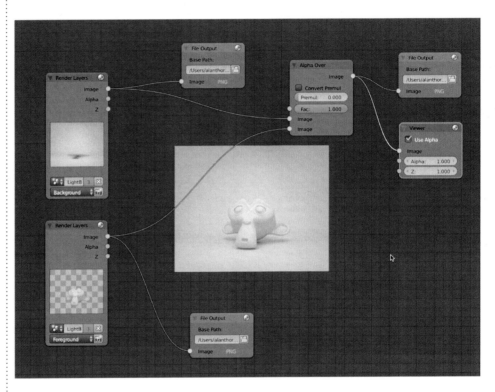

7.11 Light Portals

Calculating accurate scene lighting accounts for a substantial amount of render time. One of the reasons is that the renderer must trace light rays outward from the camera and into the scene, bouncing on the geometry, to determine intersections. This influences lights and darks, as well as the color of objects in renders. You can help Blender optimize light calculations and substantially reduce render time by using a new feature called *light portals*. In short, a light portal is a dummy light that can be positioned and sized to approximate the surface area of key light sources in the scene. This is important because it signifies to Blender the location and size of light sources, allowing the renderer to optimize lighting calculations because it no longer needs to search for lights itself. ►7.62

7.62

7.63

To get started at using light portals, create a new *area light* in the scene. To do this, open the Tools panel, switch to the *Create* tab, and create an area light. ▶**7.63**

By default, the area light is created as a regular light. This should be converted into a light portal. To achieve this, switch to the *Light* tab from the *Properties* window, and activate the check box *Portal*. Doing this deactivates the standard light behavior, transforming the object into a portal. ▶**7.64**

7.64

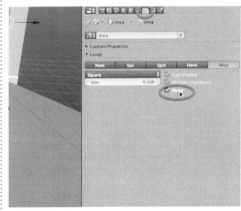

Next, use the *Rectangle* field to size the area light in *X* and *Y*, from the *Light* tab, to approximate openings in the scene (like windows and cracks) through which light travels or shines to illuminate objects in the interior. You may need to create multiple light portals if the scene has multiple light sources. Don't forget to position the light appropriately too. ▶**7.65**

7.65

And that's it! By marking area lights as portals for areas of light sources, you can substantially improve the quality of renders while maintaining the number of samples. This is because portals guide Blender on how best to optimize scene rendering.

8

Add-Ons

This chapter considers a wide and varied range of freely available Blender Add-Ons that are easy to access and install. These extend or enhance Blender's functionality and are considered in no particular order. There are many add-ons available, most free and some commercial. This chapter considers only free options. This is not because the commercial add-ons are not functional, helpful, or impressive, but because I want to restrict our exploration to add-ons available for every budget, large or small. Here, we'll see add-ons that give us access to more objects, materials, assets, and workflows, as well as add-ons that offer completely new editors or functionality. So let's get started.

8 Add-Ons

8.1 More Objects!

Blender ships with a selection of basic primitives that can be added to a scene at the touch of a button, via the *Tools* panel or *Add* menu. This includes Planes, Cubes, Circles, Spheres, Cylinders, Cones, a Torus, and a Monkey. These objects are created for more refined modeling and editing rather than for their own sake, with the possible exception of the monkey head. However, you can expand the range of objects available to you by using the *Extra Objects* add-on. To activate the add-on, select *File > User Preferences* from the application menu, and switch to the *Add-ons* tab, and then search for *extra objects*. Once located, activate the check boxes for both add-ons found (*Add Curve: Extra Objects* and *Add Mesh: Extra Objects*) and enable the add-ons. ▶8.1

8.1

After activating the add-ons, you can access more meshes by choosing *Add > Mesh* from the 3D menu. New options include *Single Vert* for creating meshes with one starting vertex, *Rounded Cube*, *Pipe Joints*, *Teapot*, *Diamonds*, and more. ▶8.2

8.2

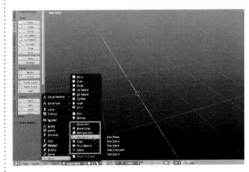

You also get additional options for creating curves and splines too. These are available from the *Add > Curve* from the 3D menu. They include *Curve Profiles*, *Spirals*, *Torus Knot Plus*, etc. ▶8.3

8.3

Another great feature about *Extra Objects* is the extent to which created objects can be customized parametrically. After creating an object, you can tweak many settings from the *Tools* panel to change it. For gear meshes, for example, you tweak *Radius* settings, *Number of Teeth*, *Width*, and more. For pipes, you can control *Length*, *Divisions*, *Angle*, and more. Each object type ships with its own specific group of settings. Try them out …. ▶8.4

8.4

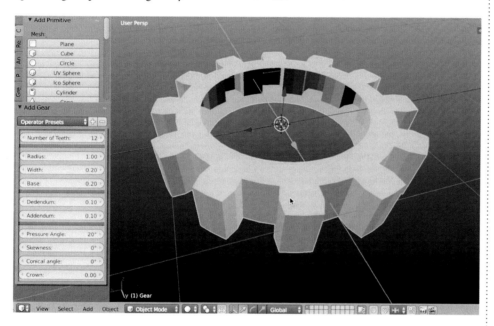

8.2 Image Planes

There are many ways to get reference images into Blender and visible in the viewport, including *Viewport Background Images* and *Empty Objects*. Another way, however, that's quick and easy is to use *Image Planes*. This feature can be enabled in Blender by activating the *Images as Planes* add-on. This add-on allows the import of an image or movie file, after which Blender constructs a plane object in the scene with a matching aspect ratio that is automatically UV mapped to the imported image. To activate this add-on, open the *User Preferences Window* by choosing *File > User Preferences* from the application menu.

8 Add-Ons

8.5 Switch to the *Add-ons* tab, and search for *images as planes*. Then, activate the add-on from the search results by enabling its check box. ▶8.5

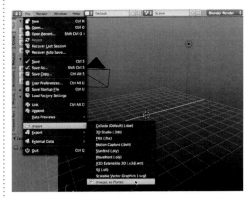

8.6 You can access the *Images as Planes* import feature from the application menu, by choosing *File > Import > Images as Planes*. ▶8.6

8.7 When selected, the Import Images as Planes dialog appears, allowing you to select a file (or *multiple* files!) to import and then to customize how the resultant planes are constructed. The *Tools* panel offers many settings for controlling the plane and its generated material. For reference planes used to guide modeling, you'll want to activate the *Shadeless* option, preventing the material from being affected by scene lighting. ▶8.7

After importing your image planes, don't forget to enable *Material* mode for *Viewport Shading*. This lets you preview the plane with its material applied in the viewport. If you're using the Plane for reference, you'll probably want to deactivate object selection using the *Outliner Window*. ▶8.8

8.8

8.3 F2 Add-On

Here's a useful add-on that has a very dedicated purpose, the *F2 Add-On*. In short, this add-on offers an intelligent and quick way to fill faces in a model. Normally, to generate a face between two edges you'll need to select opposing edges, and then choose the *Make Face* option. This option works well, but can get tedious when you need to fill many faces like this. F2 simply requires you to repeatedly press *F* on the keyboard, and it does much of the work for you by intelligently finding faces to fill. Sometimes, it gets it wrong, but in many cases the add-on can save you time.

Let's consider an example. First, activate the add-on by opening *User Preferences*, selecting *File > User Preferences* from the application menu. Switch to the *Add-ons* tab and search for *f2*, and then activate the add-on. When you do this, nothing tangible happens to the Blender interface. ▶8.9

8.9

8.10

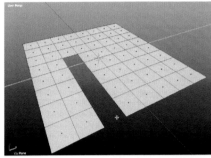

Next, consider a model in which some faces must be created between edges. This scenario can easily happen during modeling, after cutting, moving, and deleting faces. ▶8.10

8.11

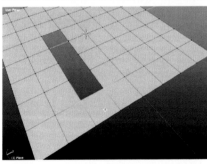

To fill this mesh using the F2 add-on, start by selecting two opposing vertices in the edges to be filled. And then press *F*. When you do this, an edge is connected between the vertices. ▶8.11

8.12

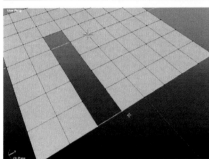

Next, hover the mouse cursor over the area where a face should be generated in the mesh, guiding the F2 add-on as to the direction of the fill. Then, press *F* again to produce the first face. ▶8.12

8.13

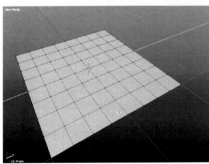

Now, repeatedly press *F* to quickly fill the remaining faces in a way that's consistent with existing mesh topology. This is really a quick way to generate many faces! ▶8.13

8.4 Landscape Tool

Whether you're rendering stills, creating animations, or making games, you'll frequently need to make terrain for exterior scenes. That is, you'll need a terra-firma, such as hills, fields, rocks, mountains, and other elements representing a natural landscape. You can create a terrain manually by sculpting onto a highly tessellated plane. However, Blender offers the *ANT Landscape Tool* for quickly generating terrains. This add-on essentially creates a tessellated plane object and lets you deform parametrically by controlling a displacement noise pattern constrained within specific limits to output believable terrains. To activate the add-on, select *File > User Preferences* from the application menu, and switch to the *Add-ons* tab and search for *ANT Landscape*, and then enable the *ANT Landscape Tool* option. ▶8.14

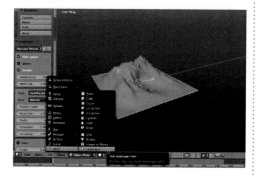

8.14

8.15

To generate a new landscape in the scene, click *Add > Mesh > Landscape* from the 3D menu. This creates a new plane object with a default deformation applied to simulate a landscape. ▶8.15

After terrain creation, you can tweak its appearance and topology directly from the Create tool bar. The ANT Landscape tool offers extensive options for customizing the landscape. Mostly important, the *Smooth* option specifies whether the landscape appears smooth or facetted, *Subdivisions* control the total number of faces in the mesh, and *Random Seed* cycles through different noise patterns to reshape the terrain. ▶8.16

8.16

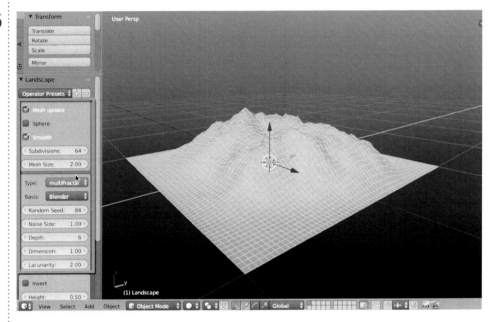

8.5 Trees and More Trees!

If you're making landscapes and exterior scenes, then you'll probably want trees. This is where the *Sapling* add-on becomes very useful. In short, *Sapling* is a tree generator add-on, which allows you to procedurally generate trees based

8.17

on initial creation parameters. By using *Sapling*, you can quickly and easy create many different types of trees. To activate the add-on, select *File > User Preferences*, and switch to the *Add-ons* tab and search for *Sapling*. Then, activate the *Sapling* add-on. ▶8.17

Once activated, create a new tree by choosing *Add > Curve > Add Tree* from the 3D menu. Selecting this creates a spline-based, tree-shaped curve in the scene. By default, the generated curve has no width or depth, and no associated geometry. It exists only as a spline. ▶8.18

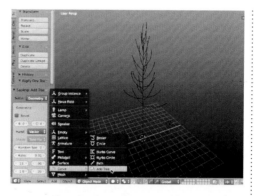

8.18

Once generated, the tree can be customized from the *Create* panel. To quickly generate geometry around the spline, enable the *Bevel* check box. The depth, radius, and prominence of the geometry are based on the remaining settings. ▶8.19

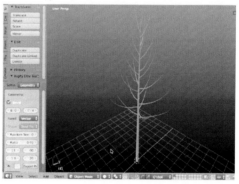

8.19

The *Random Seed* field is useful for randomizing and radically changing the shape and form of a tree. The *Scale* controls the overall size of a tree, and *Radius Scale* defines the bulkiness of the trunk. ▶8.20

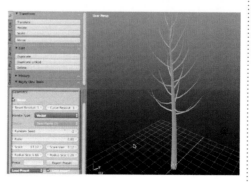

8.20

8.6 Pie Menus

If you use Maya and enjoy its radial menus and Hotbox, then you'll be delighted to find that Blender supports this system too. Pie Menus provide you with context-sensitive menus, presented in radial configuration around the subject,

8 Add-Ons

8.21

and you can quickly select options just by gesturally moving your mouse in the direction of the option. This makes switching between mesh modes (object mode, edit mode, sculpt mode, etc.) very fast. To activate Pie Menus, access the *User Preferences Window* and switch to the *Add-ons* tab. From there, search for *pie menu* and enable the *Pie Menus* option. ▶8.21

Once enabled, you can start accessing *Pie Menus* right away. Just select an object in the scene, and press the *Tab* key on the keyboard to mode switch. This time, however, on pressing time, a *Pie Menu* displays giving you access to many mode-switching options. ▶8.22

8.22

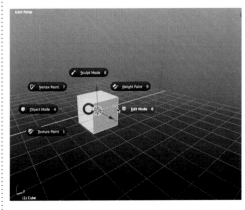

8.7 Camera Navigation

Some people don't like working with lots of keyboard shortcuts, especially for switching between cameras and viewport angles. You can solve this by activating the *Camera Navigation* add-on. This add-on creates a new tab in the *Tools* panel, giving

8.23

you clickable access to many different camera operations for the viewport. Let's install this add-on by clicking *File > User Preferences* from the file menu, to access the *User Preferences Window*. From here, switch to the *Add-ons* tab, and search for *3D Navigation*. Then, from the search results, activate the *3D Navigation* add-on. ▶8.23

After activating the *3D Navigation* add-on, open the *Tools* panel, and you'll find a *Navigation* tab. Select the *Navigation* tab, and you'll be presented with many camera pre-sets, which you can click to engage. ▶8.24

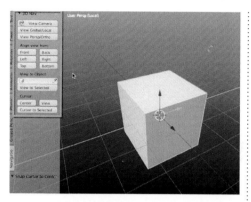

8.24

In addition to camera operations (such as *Front*, *Left*, *Back*, *Right*, *Top*, and *Bottom*), you also get 3D *Cursor* options. This includes *Center* (for snapping the 3D Cursor to the World Origin), *View* (for centering the viewport on the 3D Cursor), and *Cursor to Selected* (for moving the 3D cursor to the selected object). ▶8.25

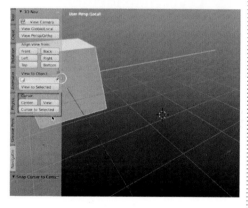

8.25

8.8 Scene Information

The Blender information panel at the top of the interface can tell you a lot about a scene, including the total and selected number of vertices, edge, and faces, as well as the memory consumption of the currently open file. But, if you need more precise information about how these data are distributed across specific kinds of objects, such as Meshes, Cameras, and Empty objects, then you'll need the *Scene Information* add-on.

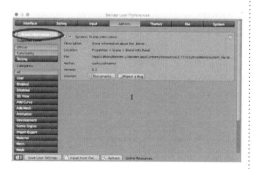

8.26

Let's activate this add-on. To do that, choose *File > User Preferences* from the application menu, and switch to the *Add-ons* tab. From there, search for *Scene Information*, and then activate the *Scene Information* add-on. ▶8.26

8 Add-Ons

8.27

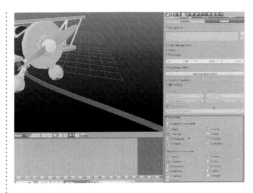

To view Scene Information, switch to the Properties window and open the Scene tab. Scroll to the bottom and expand the *Blend Info* rollout. This panel includes scene information that lists how many types of objects are included in the scene. ▶8.27

8.9 Layer Management

Every Blender Scene features a total of 20 layers, which can be viewed in isolation or together. Any object in a scene must exist within a specific layer, and this helps us for organizing scenes. However, there seems no good reason as to why layers are limited to 20, and the UI presentation of layers can be unintuitive. Blender doesn't let you rename layers and you can't tell what's on a layer except by

8.28

showing it in the viewport. Because of this, the *Layer Management* add-on was developed to enhance layer functionality within the Blender interface. To activate the add-on, select *File > User Preferences* from the application menu, switch to the *Add-ons* tab and search for *Layer Management*, and then activate the add-on. ▶8.28

To access the *Layer Management* features, click the *Layers* tab from *Tools* panel. This panel lists all layers in the scene presented in a traditional vertical stack.

In addition, by using the *Name* fields, you can rename each layer to something meaningful, describing the contents of the layer. ▶8.29

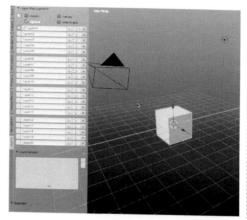

8.29

In addition to naming and renaming layers, you can toggle their visibility, disable object selection, and assign the selected objects to the selected layer. ▶8.30

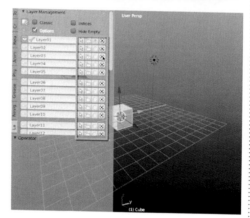

8.30

There's also a really great feature called *Layer Groups*, which works much like *Layer Comps* in Photoshop. *Layer Groups* lets you save all layer settings, arrangements, and visibility to a Group, which can be toggled on and off. In this way, you can save all layer visibility settings to a pre-set, helping you show and hide groups of layers in one click. ▶8.31

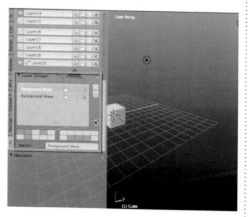

8.31

8.10 Blend File Packaging

You'll frequently need to exchange data with other artists, sending your blend files and receiving theirs. With the rise of cloud storage and version control for artistic

8.32

projects, there are many options available for those with fast Internet connections. But if you prefer offline workflows, you can easily package your blend file and its dependencies into a single ZIP file, which can be sent to others. To achieve this, you can use the *Blend File Utils* Add-On. To activate the add-on, select *File > User Preferences* from the application menu, and open the *Add-Ons* tab. From here, Search for *Blend File Utils*, and then enable the *Blend File Utils* Add-On. ▶8.32

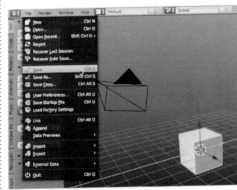

8.33

Before using the *Add-On*, your Blender Scene, and all associated texture and data, needs to be saved. Simply click *File > Save* from the application menu, and assign the file a meaningful name to save the Blender Scene. If you have unsaved textures in the UV Image Editor, you'll need to save those too with *Image > Save Image*, from the UV Image Editor menu. ▶8.33

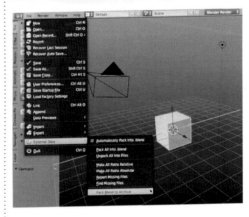

8.34

Now you can save the Blend File to a ZIP archive by choosing *File > External Data* from the application menu, and then select *Pack Blend to Archive*. Once selected, choose a file name and location, and your Blender project is packed to a ZIP file. ▶8.34

8.11 Dynamic Space Bar

Blender has many options scattered across many different menus, panels, and windows. Some options, even, are only accessible via keyboard shortcuts and have no corresponding menu entries! You can, however, distil many commonly used options into one, unified menu that is easily accessible, by using the *Dynamic Space Bar* add-on. To activate this, choose *File > User Preferences* to display the *User Preferences* Window. Then open the *Add-Ons* tab, and search for the *Dynamic Space Bar*. Finally, check the *Dynamic Space Bar* add-on to enable it. ▶8.35

8.35

You can display the *Dynamic Space Bar* menu at any time in the 3D Viewport by pressing the *Space Bar* key on the keyboard. From here, you have quick and easy access to many important options. For example, the Add Object Menu gives you direct access to the equivalent Add menu, letting you create objects in the scene, like cubes, spheres, and monkey heads. ▶8.36

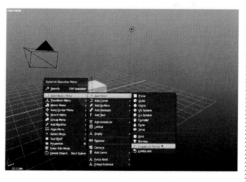

8.36

In addition, you can add modifiers to the selected object, and even snap the 3D cursor to specific locations in the scene. ▶8.37

8.37

8.12 OpenStreetMap

OpenStreetMap is a free, community-driven project to create an editable map of the world down to the level of streets. It is accessible via the website *openstreetmap.org*, and by using the site you get a topographical view of streets in almost any chosen area of the world. One interesting feature of OpenStreetMap is not only the ability to add places of interest, but to export map data to XML data files, which can, potentially, be fed into other software for processing and examination. But, it also has creative purposes too. As we'll see... ▶8.38

8.38

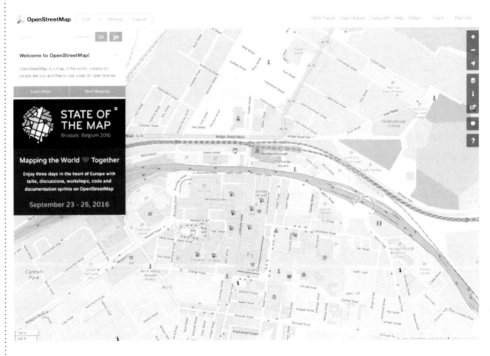

If you want to create a cityscape in Blender, or a street layout for a real world location, you can by using the OpenStreetMap add-on. This add-on allows you to import street-layouts from map data on OpenStreetMap into Blender, and Blender can generate meshes based on the layout. The generated meshes are typically flatted planes shaped and sized to match the imported street layout, and you can extrude the geometry to create buildings and cityscapes easily. The OpenStreetMap add-on is not part of the official build, but you can download and install it separately. To do that, navigate your web browser to http://wiki.openstreetmap.org/wiki/Blender. From here, you can download the OpenStreetMap plug-in from GitHub. Simply download the file *io_import_scene_osm.py*. ▶8.39

8.39

Once downloaded, you need to install and activate the plug-in within Blender. To do that, access the User Preference Dialog by choosing *File > User Preferences* from the application menu. From here, click the button *Install From File* at the bottom of the window. ▶8.40

8.40

8 Add-Ons

8.41

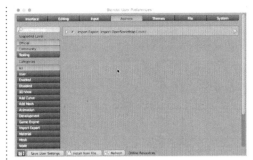

From *File-Selection* dialog, choose the downloaded file. After this, the *OpenStreetMap* add-on is shown and can be selected. ▶8.41

To use the *OpenStreetMap* add-on in Blender for generating a cityscape, you'll need to visit the *OpenStreetMap* website and find a city or town region. Simply visit OpenStreetMap.org and enter the name of a town, city, or place to see its street map. ▶8.42

8.42

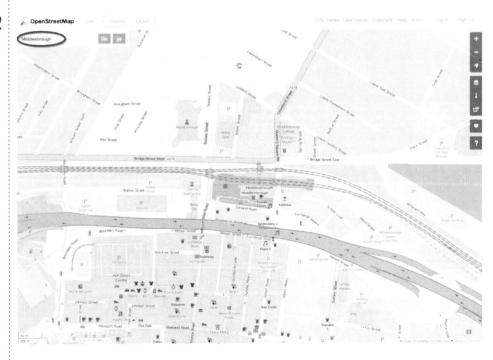

Next, click the *Export* button from the website toolbar. This prepares to export the street map information to a local file. ▶8.43

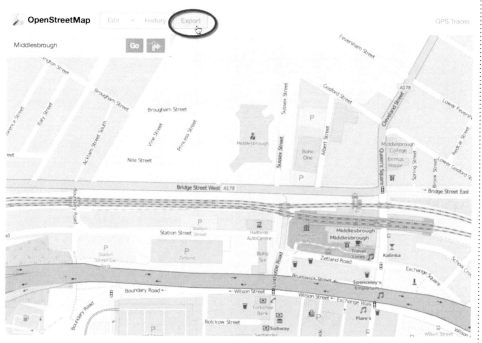

After clicking *Export*, a side panel is revealed in the webpage, which allows you to customize the map region to export. Click the button *Manually select a different area*, which lets you to box-select a region on the map to export. ▶8.44

8.45

Once you click *Manually select a different area*, you can use your mouse to click-and-drag a box-selection over the relevant area in the map to export. ▶8.45

8.46

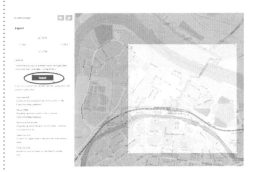

After finally selecting the street-region from the map, click the blue *Export* button in the left-hand margin (not from the top toolbar). Clicking this downloads an exported XML file to your computer, featuring all map data for the selected region. ▶8.46

8.47

Once the file has been downloaded, you may need to rename the file extension from XML to OSM, for the Blender Add-on to properly identify the file. Then, from the Blender interface, choose *File > Import > OpenStreetMap (OSM)* from the application menu. Then select the downloaded file. ▶8.47

When you do this, new and flat geometry is generated in the scene based on the imported *OpenStreetMap* data. The generated geometry matches the imported road layout from the OpenStreetMap map file. However, no depth (or height) is applied to the geometry, except in some instances where building height or terrain elevation is actually recorded in the file. ▶8.48

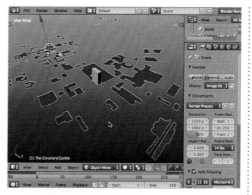

8.48

To build a randomized cityscape from the street layout, by generating buildings, you should enter edit mode for the imported mesh, and then choose *Select > Random* from the 3D Menu to randomly select faces in the model. ▶8.49

8.49

You can tweak the randomized face selection from the *Tools* panel, by using the *Percent* field (to specify the maximum proportion of faces that can be selected), and the *Seed* field to change the random selection. ▶8.50

Then just extrude the random faces upwards to create the height for the buildings. To do this, press *Alt + X* on the keyboard, or choose

8.50

8.51

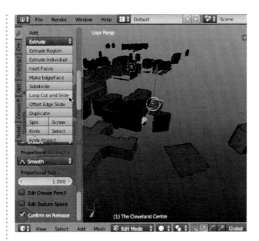

Extrude Individual from the *Tools* Panel. And voila! You now have a cityscape matching the imported road layout. Great work! ▶8.51

8.13 Easy FX—Special Effects

Post-Processing refers to the image adjustments made to a render after it's created. These adjustments include color correction, blurs, color grading, sharpening, and more. These effects can be made via a node network in the compositor, or in image editing software like Photoshop or GIMP. Frequently, post-processing requires lots of node-editing work. And the *Easy FX* Add-On simplifies that work by giving you access to a set of "out of the box" node networks, which are ready to be added to the graph for creating common effects, like Vignettes. *Easy FX* is free, and can be accessed from the website: http://www. rymdnisse.net/download/blender-addons/easyfx/ ▶8.52

8.52

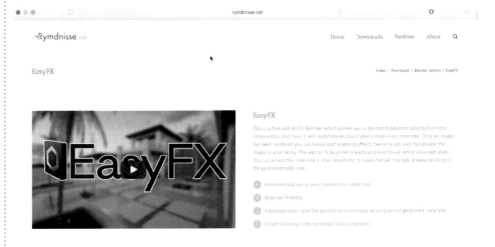

Click the *Download* button to download the *EasyFX* Python Script (add-on) to your computer. Once downloaded, install the add-on by choosing *File > User Preferences* from the application menu to access the *User Preferences* Dialog. From the *Add-Ons* tab, choose *Install from File*. Then select the add-on file to install. ▶8.53

8.53

After enabling the *Easy FX* add-on, Click *Render* to see the fully rendered result of your scene in the *UV Image Editor*. From this Editor, open the *Tools* tab, and then click the *Easy FX* tab to view all options included with the Add-On. ▶8.54

8.54

From here, you can apply *Cel Shading* and cartoon effects from the *Styles* tab. And you can apply *Curve* adjustments and contrast effects from the *Color* tab. As you make changes to the settings, the *Easy FX* add-on automatically generates a new node network, which is viewable from the *Node Editor* in *Compositor* mode. ▶8.55

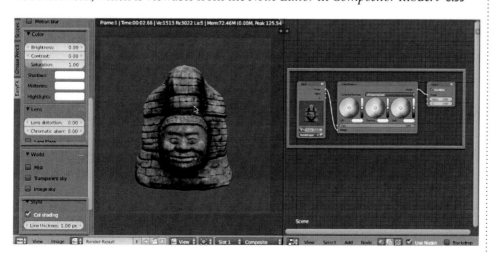

8.55

8.56

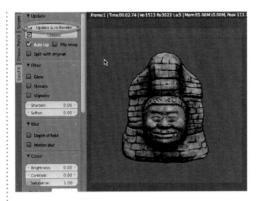

Some effects are applied in real-time and update automatically in the Image Editor. Other effects, however, require a complete re-render. You can quickly re-render the scene using the *Easy FX* Add-On, by clicking the *Update & re-Render* button from the top of the *Tools* Panel. ▶8.56

8.14 Books

Many types of scenes need books, from dusty magician towers to modern living rooms with book shelves. Books are an interesting prop and model, like junk and debris. They frequently appear in the background, together in clusters, and yet take some time to model and UV Map properly. Creating a scene with lots of books, therefore, can represent a substantial time-investment. With this in mind, the Blender Book Generator add-on makes it easy to fill a scene with many types,

8.57

of different types, and complete with UV Mapping. To access the Book Generator add-on, visit the website: https://oweissbarth.de/software/book-gen-blender-addon/ ▶8.57

8.58

Once the ZIP file is downloaded, you can integrate it into Blender from the *User Preferences* menu. Choose *File > User Preferences* from the application menu, and open the Add-Ons tab. From there, click the *Install From File* button, and choose the downloaded ZIP. Blender automatically scans its contents, and adds the Add-On to the Add-On list. ▶8.58

How to Cheat in Blender 2.7x

To generate books in the scene, choose *Add > Mesh > Add Books* from the 3D Menu. This generates a single, default book at the world origin. ▶8.59

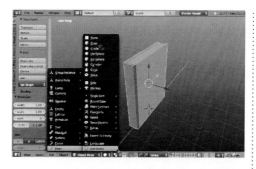

8.59

If you need to populate a book shelf really quickly, just increase *Width* field from the *Tools* Panel. As the value increases, more books are added, each with unique properties, such as width, height, and depth. This helps add variety and believability to your book shelves. ▶8.60

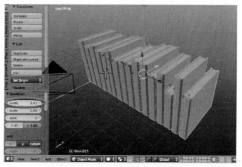

8.60

All generated books are automatically assigned UV Mapping. This makes it easy to overlay photographs and book images to the objects. ▶8.61

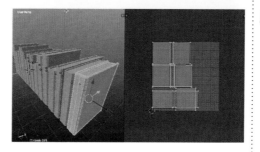

8.61

9

Game Development Cheats

Blender is a popular 3D application for game developers, especially indie developers seeking professional-grade results while working on a limited budget. Blender is a uniquely positioned application for game developers. Not only is it a free and open source, but it also offers many tools and features for creating, mapping, and exporting 3D models to industry-standard formats. It's only in the arena of image-editing tools, like layers and nondestructive pixel editing, that Blender may be regarded as truly lacking, from a holistic view. In any case, Blender is now so firmly entrenched in indie game development as a key development tool that a chapter dedicated to this subject is clearly justified. In this chapter, we consider the ways in which game developers can optimize their workflow by using Blender for making game-ready assets.

> **NOTE**
>
> This chapter does *not* focus on the Blender game engine. Rather, it examines Blender as an asset creation tool, useful for exporting completed assets (e.g., models and textures) from the application and into a third-party engine, like Unity or Unreal.

9 Game Development Cheats

9.1 Standardize Units

After running Blender, you'll probably want to tweak some settings and options for the active scene, in order to support a better game development workflow. Most game engines, like Unity and Unreal, measure world space in meters—a metric system. Consequently, Blender should be configured to match this system of units, to allow for easier referencing and sizing of objects between Blender and your game engine. It always makes sense to establish consistency in measurement and units, unless you've a very good reason not to. To do this, switch to the *Scene* tab from the *Properties* window, and from the *Units* rollout, enable the option *Metric*. ▶9.1

9.1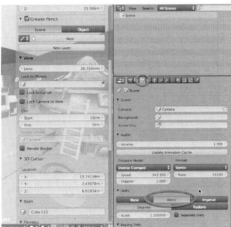

9.2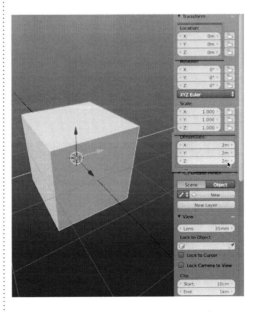

Once enabled, you can confirm that the option has taken effect simply by expanding the N Panel to view the position and size properties of the selected object. These measurements will be shown in meters. ▶9.2

9.2 Normals and Backface Culling

Game engines render graphics in real time. So it's good practice to configure your Blender viewport to match up as closely as possible with this kind of rendering. Doing this gets you real-time previews of your models directly in the Blender viewport, and these previews closely correspond to what you'd see if the models were imported into a game engine. First, game engine renderers are normally one-sided: Only one side of a polygon is rendered. This is the side corresponding to a face's normal. Blender, by default, is two-sided. This means you can see a polygon in the viewport from *both* sides, even if the Blender Internal and Cycles renderers are configured to be one-sided. Let's change viewport rendering to be one-sided. To do this, expand the N Panel inside the 3D viewport, and expand the *Shading* rollout. From there, enable the option *Backface Culling*. This ensures that polygons are rendered from only one side. ▶9.3

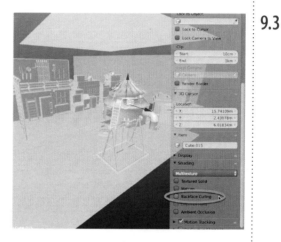

9.3

When in this display mode, a face normal becomes highly important for determining which way a face is "looking," and thus whether it's visible to the camera or not. If the face doesn't show up in the Blender viewport, then it won't show up in-engine either! To change the face direction of one or more faces, simply select them, and then choose *Mesh > Normals > Flip Normals.* ▶9.4

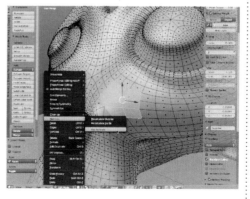

9.4

You can also get a graphical display of a mesh's normals and their direction for each face. This can be a great diagnostic tool for quickly seeing which faces would

9.5

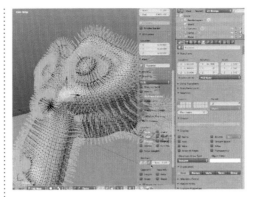

be visible to the camera, if seen. To display a mesh's normals, click the *Faces* icon from the N Panel under the *Normals* field in the *Mesh Display* rollout. ▶**9.5**

9.3 Real-Time Rendering

By default, Blender offers only solid and simplistic shading for scenes in the viewport. This doesn't match up with the sophisticated and illuminated previews you get for scenes in game engine viewports, like Unity or Unreal. Ideally, we'd like our Blender viewport to match up as closely as possible with game engine viewports in order to get the most representative real-time previews while modeling in Blender. ▶**9.6**

9.6

9.7

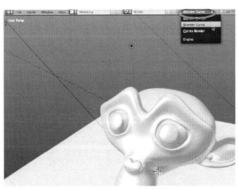

To achieve better viewport renders, switch from the Blender Internal Renderer (or Cycles) to the Game Renderer. This is specified using the *Renderer* drop-down list in the Information toolbar, in the Blender interface. ▶**9.7**

After switching to the Game Renderer, open the N Panel for the 3D viewport, and activate *GLSL* shading from the *Shading* rollout. Then, activate the

Ambient Occlusion check box to display screen space ambient occlusion for your scene. This gives you quick, real-time previews for ambient occlusion. This even displays in *Solid* mode! ▶9.8

9.8

Now let's establish a three-point lighting system to illuminate the subject more believably. We'll use the technique of "fakiosity" to simulate *global illumination*. That is, we'll use three lights of the kind *key*, *fill*, and *rim* to produce illumination on the subject that wraps around it, as real-world lighting would. This enhances the realism of the render. To get started, create a key light, using a *spotlight*. Simply, click the *Spot* button from the Blender Tools panel. ▶9.9

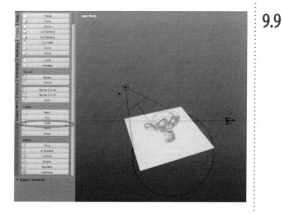

9.9

Select the newly created spotlight. This represents the key light, and it should be focused on the subject at roughly a 45-degree angle from above. From the *Light* tab in the *Properties* window, increase the *Energy* to brighten the key light—The strength value will vary depending on your scene. ▶9.10

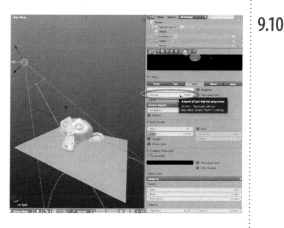

9.10

In addition to the key light just created, create a *point* light for the rim, and create a *hemi* light for the fill. The rim light should be positioned behind the subject and lower than the key light, and it should be set to a weaker intensity than the key.

9.11

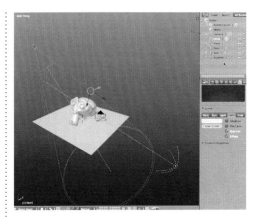

Next, the *Hemi* light should "fill" the scene with ambient light from an angle that is, normally, an averaged opposite of the key and the fill. It should also be of lower intensity than either the key or the fill, and its color will often match the sky, for an outdoor scene. ▶9.11

Now change the viewport shading mode to *Material*. This displays a fully rendered model and scene, in real time, complete with lighting and ambient occlusion. ▶9.12

9.12

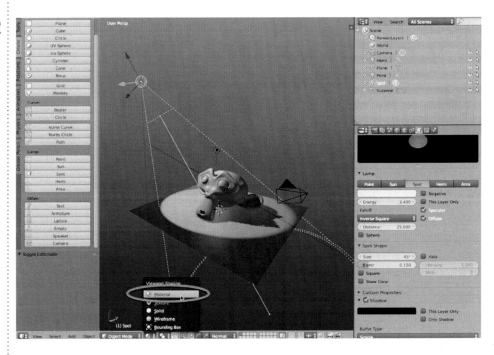

Object shadows for the key light may look rough, gritty, and awkward. You can fix this by switching to the *Light* tab from the *Properties* window and choosing

Variance for the *Buffer Type*. When you do this, shadows will look smoother and more realistic. ▶9.13

You can visualize object topology directly on the mesh in the viewport, without switching to *Wireframe* mode, by switching to the *Object Data* tab from the *Properties* window. From there, enable the check boxes *Wire* and *Draw All Edges*. ▶9.14

Voila! You now have a real-time rendered viewport for creating game models and previewing materials. It contains some default three-point lighting to simulate global illumination, giving you a more representative view of your model.

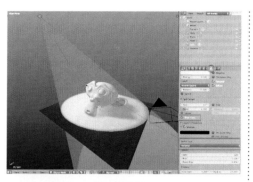

9.13

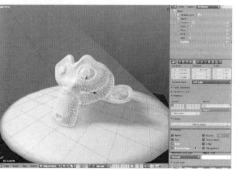

9.14

9.4 Modeling for Games: Information and Auto-Merging

Models for games should be as low poly as possible and contain as few UV seams as possible, in a way that still retains your artistic vision. Additionally, mesh topology should consist of only three- or four-sided polygons. That is, a mesh should have no *NGons* (polygons with more than four sides). In Chapter 2, we saw how to find and select NGons, and in Chapter 3, how to remove them, or at least convert them into *tris* or *quads*. We can always see how many polygons the selected model contains by viewing the Information toolbar, available by default at the top of the interface. ▶9.15

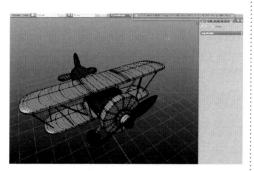

9.15

9 Game Development Cheats

Before exporting a model for a game engine, you may need to change or optimize its topology, especially if you're adapting a model from film and television for reuse in a game. This often involves combining vertices and polygons together, reducing edges wherever the mesh retains its overall shape. This reduces the number of polygons, ensuring that edges occur only where important shape changes are needed. A helpful tool in this process is *Auto-Merge Editing*, in combination with *Snapping*. To see this technique at work for reducing vertices, start by activating *Vertex Snapping*. To do this, click the *Snapping* (magnet) icon from the 3D toolbar, and for the *Snap Element*, select *Vertex* from the drop-down list. Enabling these options constrains all movement and transformations of objects to vertex increments. It's ideal for perfectly aligning one vertex to another. ▶9.16

9.16

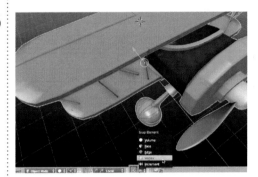

Next, enable *AutoMerge Editing*. To do this, activate *Edit* mode for the selected object, and choose *Mesh > AutoMerge Editing* from the 3D menu. When enabled, Blender automatically merges (combines) *all* vertices overlapping with each other, reducing them to one, combined vertex (assuming the overlapping vertices can be merged). ▶9.17

9.17

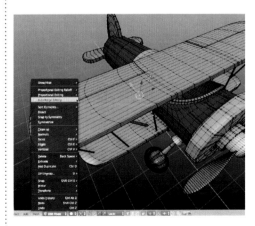

With both *Vertex Snapping* enabled and *AutoMerge Editing* activated, start moving vertices onto each other, combining them together wherever they don't contribute to the overall shape and form of the model. This will usually be in long, straight sections where tessellation is unnecessary for holding the shape. ▶9.18

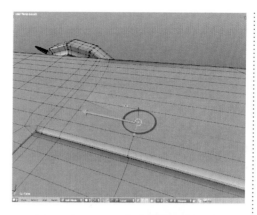

9.18

After the vertices are moved together, they will merge to form one vertex at the snapped position. By repeating this process of vertex merging, you can manually reduce polygons and edges where needed to simplify your model for a game engine. ▶9.19

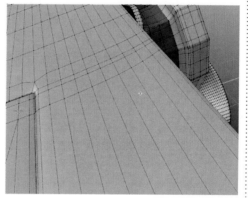

9.19

9.5 UV Seams: Visualization

UV Seams are defined, by most game engines, as the edges in a model where UV mapping pulls apart to unfold into 2D space. They effectively mark the boundaries of a UV shell or an island. UV seams, on the one hand, are essential for good unwrapping but, on the other, tend to be minimized for best performance. Unity, for example, duplicates vertices for all vertices along a seam. Consequently, increasing UV seams in a model indirectly increases the vertex count as the model is finally imported into an engine. Seams, however, can be deceptive when visualized in Blender, and this causes problems when you want

227

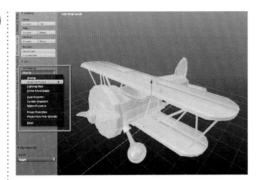

9.20

to identify where seams are and how they run in the topology. Consider, for example, unwrapping an object using *Smart UV Project*. ▶9.20

When you do this, *Smart UV Project* automatically unwraps the model, creating UV islands, all of which can be seen inside the UV Image Editor. ▶9.21

9.21

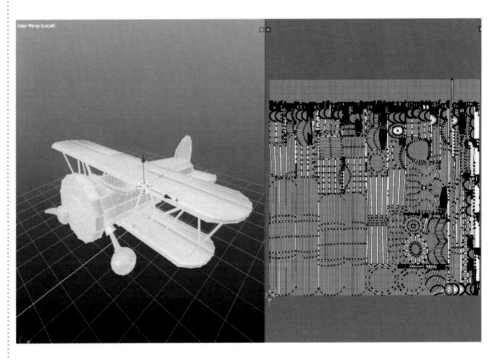

If you enable *Seams Viewing* from the 3D menu N Panel, however, you will see no seams in the model. Seams are highlighted as red edges, but Blender displays none when you unwrap with Smart UV Project. This is deceptive because although the model has seams, none are actually shown in the 3D viewport. This makes it difficult to assess how many seams are there in the model and where they're located. ▶9.22

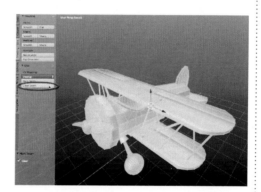

9.22

If you want to display seams in the viewport to correspond to the UV islands actually in the UV Editor, you should first clear all seams, if any are shown, by selecting all edges in the model and choosing *Clear Seam* from the *Shading/UVs* tab of the Tools panel. ▶9.23

9.23

Next, switch to the UV Image Editor, and select all UVs. Then choose *UVs > Seams From Islands* from the Image Editor menu. ▶9.24

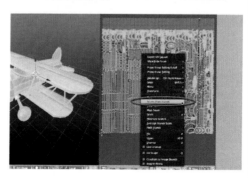

9.24

Now you'll see a clear visualization of all the seams running throughout the model. All seams are marked in red. This representation, however, only holds for the UV mapping applied at the time the *Seams From Islands* option was chosen. If you generate new mapping, you'll need to first clear the seams and then choose *Seams From Islands* again to update the display.

9.6 UV Seams: Combining Islands

Smart UV Project and other automatic-mapping methods make a good foundation and starting point for more optimized mapping. After applying an unwrap, UVs often need refinement and tweaking. For game models, for example, Smart UV Project normally produces more islands than necessary. You'll need to reduce these by combining two or more islands together into larger islands, repeating this process until you've reduced the islands to a sensible number consistent with your needs. The UV Image Editor offers tools for this purpose. Let's see them. We'll start by assuming you've just applied a Smart UV Project and are left with too many islands. ▶9.25

9.25

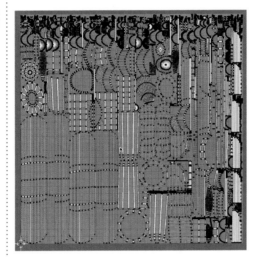

9.26

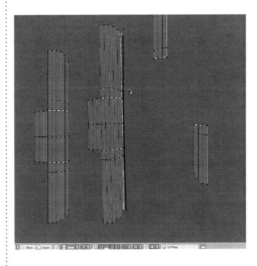

With an unwrap created, you can start joining islands together. To achieve this, select a meaningful set of perimeter edges in an island, which should be connected to another set of edges on a different island. The exact edges to select naturally vary with each model. ▶9.26

After selecting a set of edges, press the *V* key on the keyboard, or choose *UVs > Stitch* from the Image Editor menu. This initiates the *Stitch* command for combining islands together by joining the edges. Initially, the *Stitch* command offers you a preview in the Image Editor, showing you how one island connects to another. It does this by drawing a preview island in green, indicating how the connecting island will join if it were stitched now. ►**9.27**

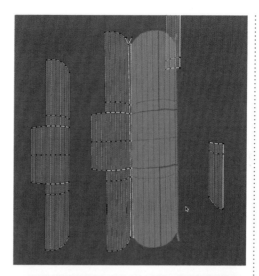

9.27

You can press the *Esc* key to reject the stitch and the *Enter* key to accept the stitch. When the stitch is accepted, the islands are connected together and become one. This reduces the seams in the model. You can repeat this process to combine more islands. ►**9.28**

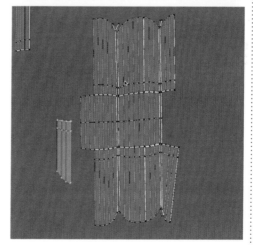

9.28

9.7 Object Combining and Modularity

Let's say you've made a table, a computer, some books, a chair, and other objects. Should these objects be exported to a game engine as separate objects (e.g., one tab, one book, and one chair)? Or as one combined object? And does it even matter technically? The answer to this question is context sensitive and worth considering. ▶9.29

9.29

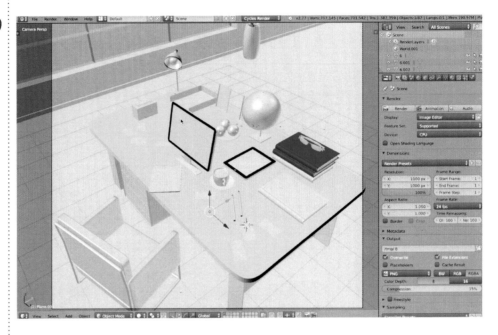

9.30

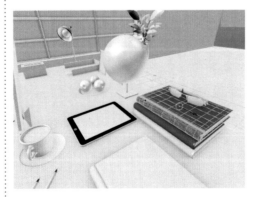

If an object (e.g., a book) should be duplicated and repeated by a level designer throughout a level in many places (to create many books), then the object should be exported as a separate object. Likewise, if an object (e.g., a book) appears in the scene a long way from a related object (e.g., a desk), then the objects should be exported as separate objects. ▶9.30

However, if objects are used only once and always appear nearby and together, and further if they have no animated separate parts, then performance benefits are often gained by exporting the objects as one, integrated mesh. You can combine objects in Blender by first selecting all the objects to combine and then using the *Join* command, available from the Tools menu. ▶9.31

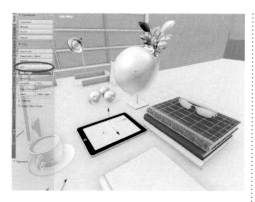

9.31

9.8 Exporting: Native versus Nonnative

So you've got a model with its final topology, UV mapping, and texturing. And now you're ready to export it to a game engine. Before exporting, however, there are some checks and final steps to perform for an optimal workflow. First, ensure your object

has a sensible pivot point, located either at its center of gravity or somewhere relevant to your needs. To change an object's pivot (*origin*) to its center of mass, select the object, and switch to the *Create* tab. Then choose *Set Origin* from the drop-down list, clicking on *Origin to Center of Mass*. ▶9.32

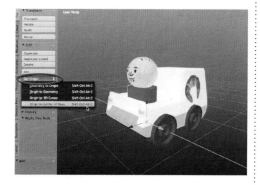

9.32

Next, make sure your object is positioned to the world origin, aligning its pivot to (*0, 0, 0*), unless you have a very good reason not to do this. If the object is not aligned to the world origin, then it'll always appear offset from where you position it. To restore an object to the world origin, expand the N Panel, and type *0, 0*, and *0* for the *X, Y*, and *Z* fields. ▶9.33

9.33

Game Development Cheats

Your object may feature *scale* and *rotation* transformations, which you probably want to keep. However, you'll want the rotation and scale fields themselves set at their defaults: *(0, 0, 0)* rotation and *(1, 1, 1)* scale. In short, you'll need to bake the scale and rotation into the model. To do this, select the model, and choose *Object > Apply > Rotation & Scale* from the 3D menu. ▶9.34

9.34

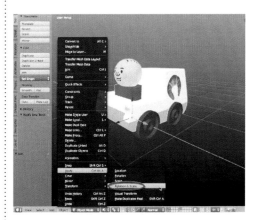

Your object may have modifiers attached on the Modifiers panel. You may or may not want these applied (baked). The export process will either bake all active modifiers or leave all modifiers unbaked, depending on your choice. Consequently, if you need to omit specific modifiers, you should deactivate them from the *Modifiers* tab where applicable. ▶9.35

9.35

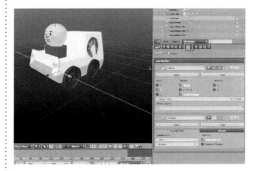

Now it's time to export your object. There are two ways to go here. First, you can save the Blender file as normal (or save a copy) to the .blend format. This is known as the *native* method because the native Blender file is saved for import to an engine. Unity supports this method, allowing you to import directly from a Blender file. But I strongly recommend avoiding this approach. The Blender file contains lots of additional data and metadata that are not needed. ▶9.36

9.36

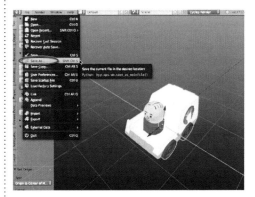

The second, and recommended method, is to use the *FBX* format. To do this, select *File > Export > FBX* from the application menu. ▶9.37

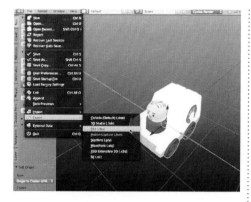

9.37

This displays an *Export* menu, from which the model and its export details can be customized. First, choose *FBX 7.4 Binary* from the Version drop-down, and enable the check box *Selected Objects* to export only the selected objects and no others. ▶9.38

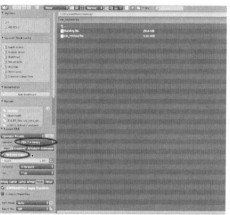

9.38

Next, select the *type* of objects within the selection to export (which can be meshes, armatures, cameras, etc.). Often this will be only *mesh* for static objects. You can select more than one option by holding the *Shift* key on the keyboard while clicking. ▶9.39

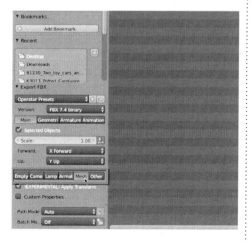

9.39

9.40

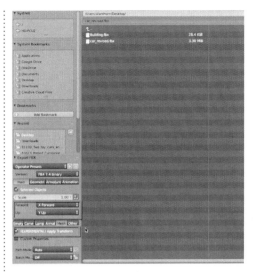

Now enable the option *Apply Transform*, and then select the appropriate settings for the *Forward* and *Up* fields. This prevents your objects from being rotated on import, due to conversions between Blender's coordinate space and the engine's coordinate space. Generally, *Y* will always be *Up*. But the *Forward* field may change depending on the direction your model is looking. ▶9.40

Finally, assign your model a name, and click the *Export FBX* button. This outputs a single FBX file, which can be imported into a game engine, such as Unity or Unreal. ▶9.41

9.41

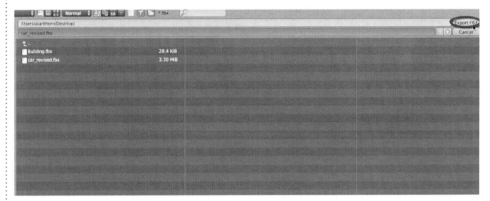

9.9 Exporting Animations

If you're exporting animated objects, from characters to cars, there are a few extra options from the FBX exporter that you should explore if you want your animations in a game engine. First, enable the *Armatures* check box from the *Export Type* list if your scene features animated skeletons. ▶9.42

9.42

Next, switch to the *Armatures* tab. Most of the default settings should work, unless you're using multiple armatures. For some character meshes to work as intended, you may need to specify *Root* for the drop-down *Armature FBXNode Type*. ▶9.43

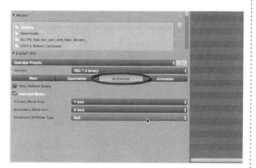

9.43

Open the *Animation* tab, ensure *Baked Animation* is enabled, as well as *Key All Bones*. These settings are important for accurately exporting animations to both Unity and Unreal Engine 4. ▶9.44

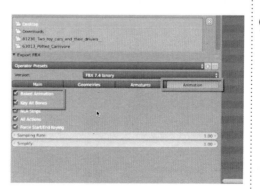

9.44

9.10 Collision Meshes

Working with complex meshes (meshes with many polygons) is common in game development. To some extent, meshes can be simplified. But there comes a point when you can't make them simpler without reducing quality in unacceptable ways. Thankfully, most engines make easy work of "crunching through" polygons, so it usually isn't a big deal that some meshes are complex. ▶9.45

However, in addition to *displaying* meshes to the gamer, the gamer needs to *collide* with meshes. You'll need collision detection to figure out when the player or nonplayer characters collide with solid objects. Mostly this is for preventing characters from walking through solids, like walls, trees, and doors. This behavior, however, requires you to have some kind of geometry to represent the object volume. You can do this with basic primitives like cubes, spheres, and capsules, but sometimes you need more complicated collision information, and you simply cannot use a complex mesh to do this. Instead, you can create a low-poly approximation of your object (a *collision mesh*). This mesh is not visible to the gamer; it simply represents an object's collision data. To achieve this, the *Decimate* modifier is available. Select your object, and from the *Modifier* tab, add the *Decimate* modifier. ▶9.46

9.45

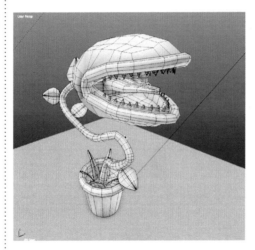

9.46

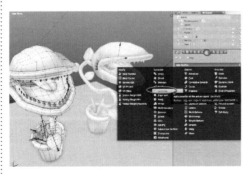

With the *Decimate* modifier added, reduce the *Ratio* field to reduce the polygons in the mesh. You can reduce the polygon count significantly, even going beyond what would be acceptable if the mesh were visible. Remember, this mesh won't be visible to the gamer. ▶9.47

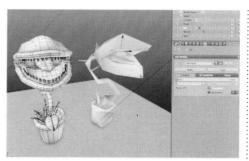

9.47

When you're satisfied, you can *Apply* the modifier and export the collision mesh as an FBX, like any regular mesh. Most engines allow you to specify a custom mesh to use as collision data. ▶9.48

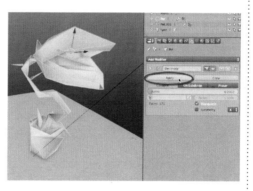

9.48

9.11 Lightmap UVs

Most game-ready meshes have at least one UV channel for an object's texture maps, but many engines let you add an additional, second channel for lightmap UVs—that is, a second and separate UV channel that contains no overlapping UVs, used for baking scene lighting to a lightmap texture. Many engines can generate these UVs for you automatically, but sometimes better mapping can be achieved by creating your own UVs. Let's see how to do that in Blender. Start by selecting your game object, which already has one UV-mapping channel. From the *Object Data* tab, there should already be one UV map listed in the *UV Maps* rollout. ▶9.49

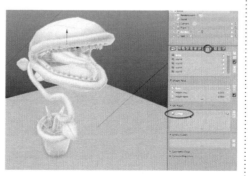

9.49

9.50

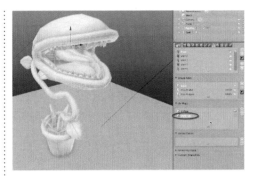

Next, create a second UV channel by clicking the + icon. A new UV channel is added to the object, but it contains no new mapping information. Double-click the UV map's name in the list to rename it. ▶9.50

To create lightmap UVs, select the object, and enter *Edit* mode, selecting all faces. From the *Shading/UVs* tab of the Tools panel, choose *Unwrap > Lightmap Pack* from the drop-down. This creates an unwrapped lightmap for the selected object. ▶9.51

9.51

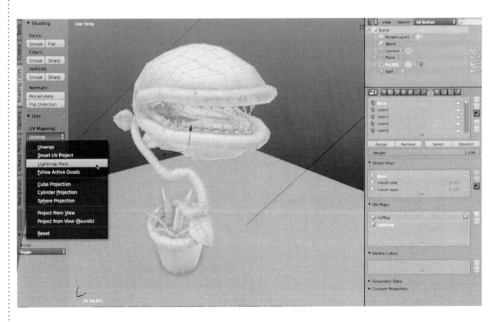

Great! Your object now has a second, lightmap UV channel, which can be activated in either Unity or Unreal to act as a lightmap channel in-engine.

9.12 Empties and Hierarchies

Remember, the scene hierarchy in Blender has value for an engine too! Specifically, the hierarchy will be preserved on export. This means you can export empty objects, lights, and cameras. These objects don't necessarily behave as functional lights and cameras in-engine, but their transformation data and relations to other objects remain intact. This is important. ▶9.52

9.52

Using hierarchies and empties, you can record the positions of cameras and other in-game objects even during animations. This makes it possible for games to dynamically append children to the empties, to include them in an animation, and the appended objects will maintain their relative offsets from the parents. To export nonrenderable objects with FBX Exporter, ensure that *Empty*, *Camera*, and *Lamp* are enabled from the *Export* dialog. These will be imported into Unity and Unreal as empty objects. ▶9.53

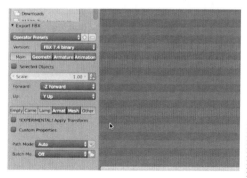

9.53

9 Game Development Cheats

9.13 Blender Export Limitations

Although game engine support for Blender is extensive, there are objects, properties, and features that simply don't export at all. Or, more specifically, there are features of Blender that, while technically exportable, are currently unsupported in most engines. They include the following:

1. *Scene and environment settings:* You can't export scene ambient lighting, fog settings, ambient occlusion, and other scene-wide properties.

2. *Constraints and modifiers:* You cannot export constraints and modifiers in their raw form. Modifiers can be baked to the mesh, saving their end results, but the modifiers and their parameters are Blender-only.

3. *Lighting and materials:* You cannot export Blender lights and their settings, and you cannot export Blender materials intact. You can export textures and then import them into a game engine to reconstruct the material in Blender, but the Blender material itself cannot be exported.

4. *Physical simulations:* You cannot export Blender physics and its effects for animations, except by baking the animation to key frames.

10

Interoperability

This chapter considers many third-party tools, services, and applications that in some way integrate with Blender. That is, they complement a Blender workflow in an important sense, enhancing your productivity. Most of these tools are free, and some are commercial. Some are stand-alone applications, and some are websites. In any case, we'll take a tour de force of the many tools "out there" that interoperate with Blender and make our lives easier.

10 Interoperability

10.1

10.2

10.1 SVG and Inkscape

Inkscape is a free, open-source vector graphics application, much like Adobe Illustrator in terms of functionality. It's used primarily for creating graphics based on editable splines and other parametric (mathematically generated) shapes. This means vector graphics can be edited, or up-sized and down-sized without any quality loss. This makes them especially useful for creating logos, web page designs, and user interfaces. ▶10.1

Graphics created with Inkscape are saved, by default, to the SVG (scalable vector graphics) format, which is an open-standard file format. Blender has the incredible ability to import SVG files. This means you can save shapes, graphics, and designs in Inkscape and then import them directly into Blender as 2D shapes and splines. From here, these designs can be converted into flat, renderable meshes. To import an SVG file into Blender, click *File > Import > Scalable Vector Graphics* from the application menu. ▶10.2

> **NOTE**
>
> Inkscape can be downloaded and installed for Windows, Mac, and Linux from its official home page at https://inkscape.org.

> **NOTE**
>
> Inkscape is not the only software that can save to SVG files. Other applications include GIMP, Photoshop, and Illustrator.

From the *Import* dialog, select an SVG file to import. Once imported, the Blender viewport may seem to contain nothing new, but the Outliner window tells us otherwise. This sometimes happens because the imported shape is very small or the viewport camera is zoomed too far for the imported shape to be immediately visible. In any case, the imported shape will be added to the scene as a *curve*—that is, a spline object. ▶10.3

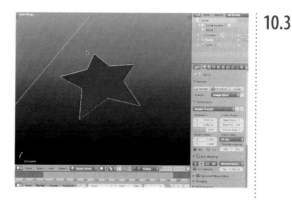

10.3

You can convert the imported curve to a regular mesh by selecting *Object > Convert To > Mesh from Curve* from the 3D menu. ▶10.4

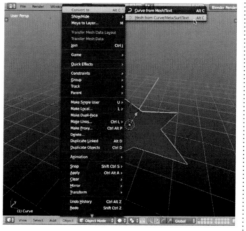

10.4

After Blender converts the curve to a mesh, the topology retains the original shape using either *tris* or *quads*. However, the edge flow may be far from ideal. Consequently, the generated mesh may require retopology. ▶10.5

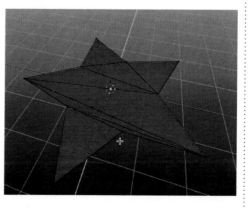

10.5

10 Interoperability

10.2 Blend Swap

Making models is an enjoyable but time-consuming art. Some models, like characters and creatures, can take a long time to design, sculpt, and retopologize. For this reason, artists often search for time-savers. One way to save time is by using a stock library of premade models. These can either be used right away or act as a starting point for something more intricate. Most stock libraries are commercial, but free ones do exist. One free example is Blend Swap (http://www.blendswap.com).

Blend Swap is a searchable online database of Blender scene files, available under different kinds of licenses that permit varied uses. These files range from single objects (e.g., tables, chairs, and characters) to complete scenes and environments (e.g., spaceship interiors, factories, and castles). With a free account, you can download and open the files in Blender. To search the website, just click *Search*, and enter your criteria. You can even filter the search by license to ensure your intended usage is permitted.

10.3 Free Images and Textures

There are many places online where you can find freely available textures and images for use in your projects. This section contains a selection that is widely used by the Blender community. For 3D modelers, we may distinguish between three types of images based on usage: (1) *textures* or *maps* (images applied to 3D objects by materials), (2) *concept art* and *reference images* (loaded into Blender to aid scene creation), and (3) *environmental images* (e.g., skies, backgrounds, and billboards), which are interwoven into a scene for special effects. For photos, references, and images, two websites are especially useful: Pixabay (https://pixabay.com/) and PixelSquid (https://www.pixelsquid.com/). Let's start with the first, Pixabay is a free, online library of public domain images (Creative Commons, or CC0). You can search for the images you need and then download the image files to your computer. Site usage requires free registration. PixelSquid, in contrast, is a searchable library of "turnaround" images. This refers to prop objects (e.g., tables, bottles, cars, etc.) that can be rotated, within the web page, to angle and perspective and then saved to a standard image file, capturing the object at the selected viewing angle.

Simply search for an object, and then click and drag the found object to rotate it to your preferred angle. Usage of the site requires a free account, and at the time of writing, many objects are free to download and use.

For textures, there are many options. Three websites are http://opengameart.org, http://www.textures.com, and http://www.mayang.com/textures/. Each of these websites contains free textures for use under different licenses and conditions. Each site offers a searchable database of textures in standard image formats, like JPG and PNG, which can be downloaded and applied to objects in Blender.

In addition to photos, references, images, and textures, you'll need HDRI Sky domes and Sky boxes to create image-based ambient lighting for your scenes, especially when rendering with Cycles. You can find some freely available 4K Skyboxes at http://hdri-skies.com, with the option to purchase larger sizes if needed.

10.4 Blender Cloud and Texture Library

More recently, the Blender Cloud website (https://cloud.blender.org/p/textures/) has emerged, which offers a free library of public domain textures that can be downloaded and integrated into your Blender scenes.

However, Blender Cloud is more than just a texture library. For a monthly subscription cost, you can get extra features, which include access to the texture library from within the Blender interface via an add-on as well as access to tutorial content and Blender projects.

10.5 Working with Colors and Color Palettes

Developing a color scheme and color palette is an important preliminary step when creating a scene. Colors tell stories, set mood, convey motion, and express ideas. By establishing a color scheme and by making decisions about color, you are deciding how your work will "talk" to the viewer. Blender offers many color-based brush tools for texture painting, both in the 3D view and in the UV Image Editor. From these views, you get access to brush tools that rely on color as their raw material. For this reason, color plays an important role when texture painting in Blender. For establishing a color scheme, according to well-established color selection rules, you can visit color scheme websites. Two notable sites are The Adobe Color Wheel (https://color.adobe.com/) and The Color Scheme Designer (http://colorschemedesigner.com). Let's see an example via The Adobe Color Wheel. This website allows you to select from a range of color selection rules. These define color-harmonizing relationships to help you pick a harmonious range of colors. ▶10.6

10.6

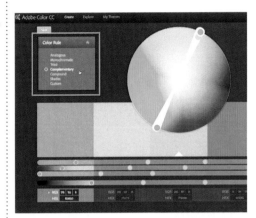

After the color rule is selected, click inside the color wheel to make a color selection. When you do this, additional colors are auto-selected, according to the rule, and are added to the color palette, presented as color squares at the bottom of the interface. Continue to tweak your color selection until the palette generated is consistent with your needs. ▶10.7

10.7

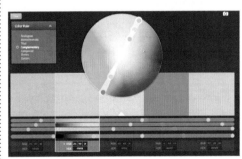

In addition to developing a color palette from scratch, you can upload an image (with a strongly developed color scheme) and have the website extrapolate a color palette from that instead. To do that, just click the camera icon at the top corner of the interface to select an image from your computer. This option is especially useful if you're working from concept art, or have found inspiration art and want to use the same color scheme. ▶10.8

10.8

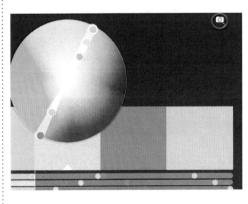

After developing the color scheme, you'll be left with five unique color swatches. You'll want to import these colors into Blender as selectable swatches for texture painting. Here's how to do that. Open the UV Image Editor, and switch to *Paint* mode to access the painting features. ▶10.9

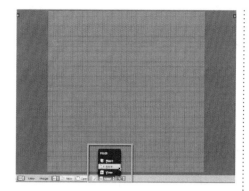

10.9

Next, open the Tools panel, and view the *Brush* tools. Select a standard *Texture Draw* brush, and then a *Circle* color picker appears underneath, allowing you to select a color. ▶10.10

10.10

The Blender painting tools feature a Color Swatch Palette, letting you build up a collection of custom color swatches. To create a new palette, click the *New* button from the *Paint* rollout. ▶10.11

10.11

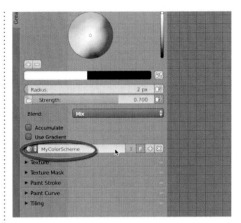

10.12

Next, assign the color scheme a unique name from the *Palette Name* field, and then press *Enter* on the keyboard to confirm the name. The + button can be clicked to add additional palettes if needed. ▶10.12

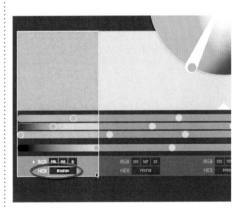

10.13

Now we must copy and paste the colors from the Adobe Color Scheme into Blender, adding the colors, one by one, to our palette for easy selection and reuse. To do this, select the first color swatch in the scheme from the Adobe Color Picker, simply by clicking it. Then click inside the *Hex* color field, and copy the hex value (with *Ctrl* + *C*, or *Cmd* + *C*). ▶10.13

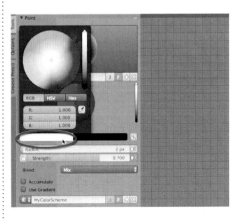

10.14

Return to Blender, and click on the Foreground Color swatch, beneath the color picker. When you do this, a color selection popup appears. ▶10.14

Switch to the *Hex* tab, and paste the color value into the type-in box. This selects the copied color from the color wheel. ▶10.15

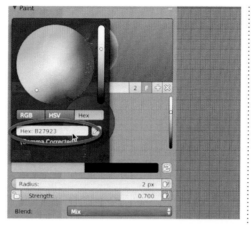

10.15

When the color is selected, click the + icon next to the color wheel to add the selected color to the active palette. On clicking this, a new color swatch block appears beneath the wheel, offering quick access to your color. ▶10.16

10.16

Repeat this process to add the remaining colors from the scheme. When this is completed, you'll have color swatches for each color, and clicking a swatch will select the chosen color for the brush. ▶10.17

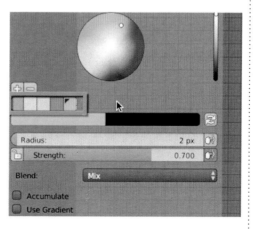

10.17

10.18

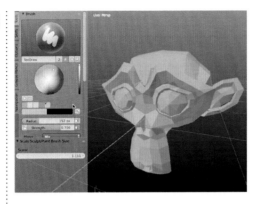

Voila! You've now established a color palette! One great quality of the Blender color palette system is its reusability across editors. Even now, if you switch to a 3D view and enter *Texture Paint* mode, to access the texture-painting features, you can still access the same color palette. Great stuff! ▶10.18

10.6 Maps and Terrain Displacement

Sometimes you'll need to build terrains and landscapes for real-world locations as accurately as possible. That is, you'll need to model places that really exist— like London, Paris, the Sahara Desert, or the Himalayas. One way to do this is to use height map terrain data (as a grayscale image) and apply the data to a tessellated plane as a displacement. You can download height map data for any world location from the website http://terrain.party. This website uses OpenStreetMap data to display a world map onto which you can make a rectangular selection, indicating the region for which height map data are needed. ▶10.19

10.19

10.20

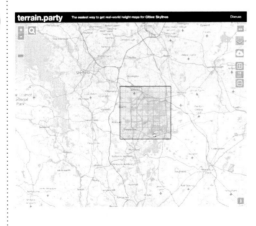

Use the mouse to click and drag a rectangular selection on the map inside the Web browser, specifying the height map data to generate. ▶10.20

Next, click the *Export* button from the right-hand margin to download the terrain data. The downloaded data include several image files, as height maps, in PNG format. These are included inside a Zip file, which should be extracted. ▶10.21

10.21

Open Blender, and import the terrain height map image (merged version). You can do this through the UV Image Editor by choosing *Image > Open Image* and then selecting the image file. ▶10.22

10.22

Next, create a new grid object in the scene. Open the Tools panel, and select *Grid* from the *Create* tab. A grid is a plane with additional subdivisions. Increase the grid scale to fill more of the scene. ▶10.23

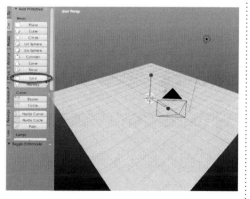

10.23

10.24

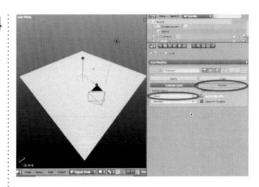

Add a *Subdivision Surface* modifier to the grid from the Modifiers panel of the *Properties* window, and set the *Subdivision Type* to *Simple*. This prevents smoothing behaviors on the geometry. Then increase the *View* subdivisions to increase the density of the plane. This is necessary to accommodate the terrain displacement details. ▶**10.24**

10.25

Now add a *Displace* modifier to the grid. This lets you deform an object, and its vertices, based on a grayscale image (height map). *Black* pixels push the terrain down to form valleys, and *White* pixels pull the terrain upward to form mountains. ▶**10.25**

10.26

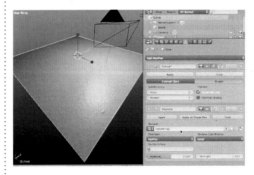

Now select the height map texture for the *Texture* slot, and the *Displace* modifier takes effect immediately on the terrain. Initially, you may not notice any effect, or the effect may be very subtle, though detectable. You can change viewport shading to *Material* or *Rendered* mode to get a better view of the bump interaction with light sources, if needed. ▶**10.26**

You can intensify the displacement on the grid by increasing the *Strength* setting in the *Displace* modifier. This is the equivalent of raising the contrast for the height map image: darkening the shadows and brightening the highlights. ▶10.27

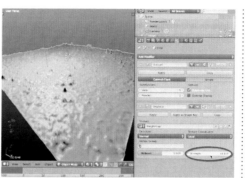

10.27

10.7 MakeHuman

MakeHuman is a freely available character generation program. By using sliders and type-ins for fields like age, height, and facial features, you can parametrically create characters quickly and easily. By default, MakeHuman does not integrate with Blender. But you can easily export from MakeHuman, transferring your character files to Blender. Let's see how. MakeHuman can be downloaded for Windows, Mac, and Linux from http://www.makehuman.org/.

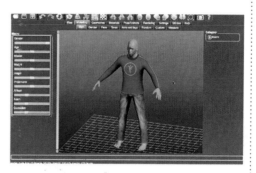

10.28

Using MakeHuman, you can quickly generate character models, complete with clothing, rigs, and animation, simply by using the application sliders and controls. ▶10.28

When you're ready to export your model, there are several ways to go. The most reliable and consistent method presently, given changes in the MakeHuman software and Blender, is to use the FBX format. To achieve this in MakeHuman, select the *Files* tab, and then select the *Export* tab. From here, choose the *FBX* file

10.29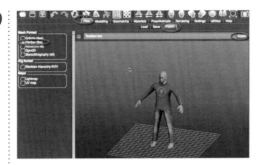

format from the left-hand margin, and then enter a name for the file. Finally, click the *Export* button to save. ▶**10.29**

10.30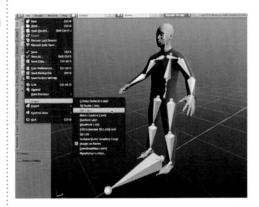

To import the character model into Blender, choose *File > Import > FBX* from the application menu, and then choose the *FBX* character from your computer. This will import all exported data, including the character mesh, clothes, textures, and rig. ▶**10.30**

10.8 Renderers: V-Ray and RenderMan

Blender ships with three main renderers: Internal, Game, and Cycles. These renderers are powerful and are suited for different purposes. However, in addition to these renderers, the powerful V-Ray and RenderMan are available as commercial add-ons. V-Ray for Blender is available from http://www.chaosgroup.com/en/2/vray_blender.html, and RenderMan is available from https://renderman.pixar.com/view/renderman4blender.

Index

Index

Index

Index

Index

Index